2

THE SPRINGS OF FLORIDA

TEXT AND PHOTOGRAPHS BY
DOUG STAMM

Contributing Photographer
Timothy T. Whitney

Line Drawings by Steve Leatherberry

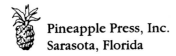
Pineapple Press, Inc.
Sarasota, Florida

To my Kira and Matthew —
that they will grow to know
the gifts of our Creator.

Inquiries should be addressed to:
Pineapple Press, Inc.
P.O. Drawer 16008
Southside Station
Sarasota, Florida 34239

CATALOGING IN PUBLICATION DATA

Stamm, Douglas R.
    The springs of Florida / Doug Stamm ; contributing photographer,
Timothy T. Whitney. — 1st ed.
        p. cm.
    Includes bibliographical references.
    ISBN 1-56164-054-9: Hb   — ISBN 1-56164-048-4: Pb
    1. Springs—Florida. 2. Natural history—Florida. I. Title.
GB1198.3.F6S73   1994
551.49'8—dc20
                                                93-33773
                                                CIP

First Edition
10 9 8 7 6 5 4 3 2 1

Design by Steve Duckett and Cynthia Keenan
Printed in Hong Kong

CONTENTS

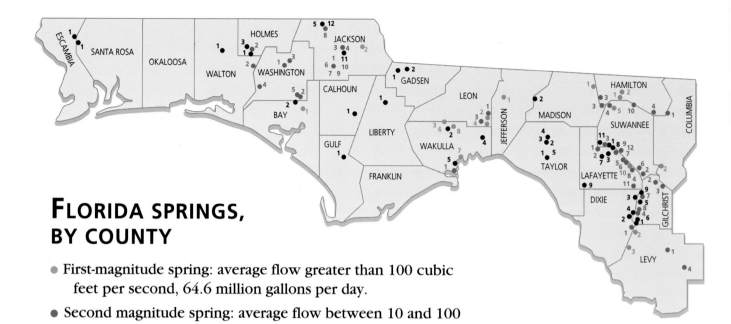

FLORIDA SPRINGS, BY COUNTY

- First-magnitude spring: average flow greater than 100 cubic feet per second, 64.6 million gallons per day.

- Second magnitude spring: average flow between 10 and 100 cubic feet per second.

- Third magnitude spring: spring flow less than 10 cubic feet per second, 6.46 million gallons per day.

★ National Forest Recreational Area

✳ State Park/Recreational Area

4. Hart Springs
5. Lumber Camp Springs
6. Otter Springs
7. Rock Bluff Springs
8. Sun Springs
9. Townsend Spring

GULF
1. Dalkeith Springs

HAMILTON
1. Alapaha Rise ●
2. Holton Spring ●
3. Morgans Spring
4. White Springs

HERNANDO
1. Bobhill Springs
2. Little Springs
3. Salt Spring
4. Weeki Wachee Spring ●

HILLSBOROUGH
1. Buckhorn Spring
2. Eureka Springs
3. Lettuce Lake Spring
4. Lithia Springs
5. Six Mile Creek Spring
6. Sulphur Springs

HOLMES
1. Jackson Spring
2. Ponce de Leon Springs ✳
3. Vortex Blue Spring

ALACHUA
1. Glen Springs
2. Hornsby Spring ●
3. Magnesia Spring
4. Poe Springs

BAY
1. Gainer Springs ●
2. Pitts Spring

BRADFORD
1. Heilbronn Spring

CALHOUN
1. Abes Spring

CITRUS
1. Blue Spring
2. Chassahowitska Springs ●
3. Crystal River Springs ●
4. Homosassa Springs ● ✳
5. Ruth Spring

CLAY
1. Green Cove Spring
2. Wadesboro Spring

COLUMBIA
1. Bell Springs
2. Ichetucknee Springs ● ✳

DIXIE
1. Copper Spring
2. Little Copper Spring
3. Guaranto Spring
4. McCrabb Spring

ESCAMBIA
1. Mystic Springs

GADSDEN
1. Chattahoochee Spring
2. Glen Julia Springs

GILCHRIST
1. Bell Springs
2. Blue Springs
3. Ginnie Spring

JACKSON

1. Black Spring
2. Blue Springs ●
3. Blue Hole Spring
4. Bosel Spring
5. Daniel Springs
6. Double Spring
7. Gadsden Spring
8. Hays Spring
9. Mill Pond Spring
10. Springboard Spring
11. Sand Bag Spring
12. Waddells Mill Pond Spring

JEFFERSON

1. Wacissa Springs Group ●
   Big Spring
   Garner Springs
   Blue Spring
   Buzzard Log Springs
   Minnow Spring
   Cassidy Spring
   Springs No. 1 and 2
   Thomas Spring
   Log Springs
   Allen Spring
   Horsehead Spring

LAFAYETTE

1. Allen Mill Pond Spring
2. Blue Spring
3. Convict Spring
4. Fletcher Spring
5. Mearson Spring
6. Owens Spring
7. Perry Spring
8. Ruth Spring
9. Steinhatchee Spring
10. Troy Spring ●
11. Turtle Spring

LAKE

1. Alexander Springs ● ★
2. Apopka Spring
3. Blue Springs
4. Bugg Spring
5. Camp La No Che Spring
6. Holiday Springs
7. Messant Spring
8. Seminole Springs

LEON

1. Horn Spring
2. Natural Bridge Spring ●

3. Rhodes Springs
4. St. Marks Spring ●

LEVY

1. Blue Spring
2. Fannin Springs ●
3. Manatee Springs ● ✳
4. Wekiva Springs

LIBERTY

1. White Springs

MADISON

1. Blue Spring ●
2. Pettis Spring
3. Suwanacoochee Spring

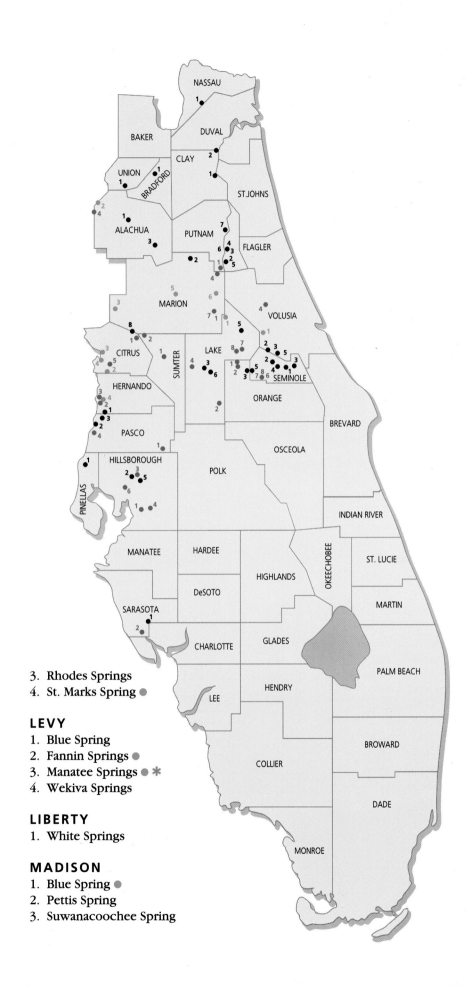

MARION
1. Juniper Springs ★
2. Orange Spring
3. Rainbow Springs ● ✳
4. Salt Springs ★
5. Silver Springs ●
6. Silver Glen Springs ● ★
7. Fern Hammock Springs
8. Wilson Head Spring

NASSAU
1. Su-No-Wa Spring

ORANGE
1. Rock Springs ✳
2. Wekiwa Springs ✳
3. Witherington Spring

PASCO
1. Crystal Springs
2. Horseshoe Spring
3. Magnolia Springs
4. Salt Springs

PINELLAS
1. Health Spring

PUTNAM
1. Beacher Springs
2. Mud Spring
3. Nashua Spring
4. Satsuma Spring
5. Forest Spring
6. Welaka Spring
7. Whitewater Springs

SANTA ROSA
1. Chumuckla Springs

SARASOTA
1. Little Salt Spring
2. Warm Mineral Springs

SEMINOLE
1. Clifton Spring
2. Elder Springs
3. Health Springs
4. Lake Jessup Spring

5. Miami Springs
6. Palm Springs
7. Sanlando Springs
8. Starbuck Spring

SUMTER
1. Fenney Springs
2. Gum Springs

SUWANNEE
1. Bonnet Spring
2. Branford Springs
3. Charles Springs
4. Ellaville Spring
5. Falmouth Spring ●
6. Little River Springs
7. Peacock Springs ✳
8. Royal Spring
9. Running Springs
10. Suwannee Springs
11. Thomas Spring
12. Tilford Spring

TAYLOR
1. Carlton Spring
2. Ewing Spring
3. Hampton Springs
4. Iron Spring
5. Waldo Springs

UNION
1. Worthington Spring

VOLUSIA
1. Blue Spring ● ✳
2. Gemini Springs
3. Green Springs
4. Ponce de Leon Springs ✳
5. Seminole Spring

WAKULLA
1. Crays Rise
2. Indian Springs
3. Kini Spring ●
4. Newport Springs
5. Panacea Mineral Springs
6. River Sink Spring ●
7. Spring Creek Springs ●
8. Wakulla Springs ● ✳

WALTON
1. Euchee Springs
2. Morrison Spring

WASHINGTON
1. Beckton Springs
2. Blue Spring
3. Cypress Spring
4. Blue Springs
5. Williford Spring

ACKNOWLEDGMENTS

Many individuals have contributed greatly to the preparation of this book. At its conception and through early and difficult travels and dives, Tim Whitney played an invaluable role in the effort to obtain information and photographs. He joins me in extending appreciation to Dr. Carter Gilbert of the University of Florida and Dr. Ralph Yerger of Florida State University for species identification and information that was freely provided and to Dr. Larry Briel who served as underwater guide in Wakulla Springs. I regret that the late Dr. Archie Carr cannot see this long project completed as he did much to ensure the accuracy of the original manuscript.

The management and staff of Silver, Wakulla, Homosassa, and Weeki Wachee springs generously granted us access to dive and photograph their springs. We are indebted to them and to the mermaids of Weeki Wachee for their assistance and interest in this work.

Also to Steve Leatherberry, dive partner and artist of the perceptive illustrations included here; diving partner and brother Trace, who shared many initial responsibilities; to Sue Allen and Lois Schuren, proficient in their skills in helping to prepare the manuscript; and to the many anonymous divers and travelers met along the springs who so often served to point the way — to all these friends, we say thanks.

To Dr. Ross Horrall of the University of Wisconsin–Madison Marine Studies Center and to J. Phillip Keillor of the Sea Grant Institute – University of Wisconsin, I extend my appreciation for their patient regard for my wanderings long ago.

Far from least important, to my mother and father, Wayne and Darlyne Stamm, who first showed a boy the ocean's edge, I am grateful. And most importantly, my thanks to my dear wife Lucy, who said she'd still love me whether this book ever got published or not.

PREFACE

This book was begun in Peacock Springs on my first dive into the springs of Florida more than 15 years ago. What I saw convinced me the world should know these places better.

Not long after, while researching information already known about Florida's springs, I happened across the classic writings of William Bartram, who, in his book *Travels*, wrote with eloquent awe of his encounters with the springs of Florida, these very same springs that now captivate us more than two centuries later. Impressed by the accuracy of his insight, and moved by his reverent and open innocence, I have wondered what would flow from Bartram's pen if he could weave in a weightless journey through the depths of those transparent waters with the ease we do today. It is appropriate that he introduces each chapter of this book as his prose still best describes the wondrous nature of these places.

The photographs collected here were obtained over a 15-year period at spring sites throughout Florida. They are the result of hundreds of hours underwater, during both night and day, in springs large and small, and at varying seasons of the year.

There is a simple beauty endemic to the springs of Florida. They attract increasing numbers of us yearly to their quiet pools and transparent streams. In our journeys there, many of us have sought to better understand their origins, to visit their deeper, hidden realms, and to know their many inhabitants. For those who have entered their waters or, from the surface, viewed their crystalline expanses with inquisitive wonder, I have attempted to reveal their hidden places and creatures.

One book cannot portray all the spring environments of Florida and the creatures inhabiting them. Some inhabitants are too rare, some too remote, and others too fleeting to be included here. Rather, this is a passing view of the spring environments above and below the water and represents but momentary events in the life history of underwater inhabitants most likely to be encountered by visitors there. Not all springs will contain all of the creatures presented here. Many will contain more. There remain many springs and inhabitants not included in this collection.

The many realms of fresh water that most often surround us are dark rivers, clouded ponds, and the opaque depths of inland lakes. We cannot see into them nor fathom the incessant activities of life that occur throughout their depths. The many springs that jewel the landscape of Florida are ornate exceptions to an environment so often veiled in obscurity. They are translucent openings into a dominion very rare: a crystalline world of fresh water at the edge of the sea.

Doug Stamm
Blue Springs Camp

The early mist of dawn brings primeval tranquility to Peacock Springs, its crystalline blue pool almost hidden among ancient lowland cypress. Its water rising from more than five miles of underground passageways, it flows slowly for more than a mile to the Suwannee River.
Peacock Springs State Recreation Area, Suwannee County

INTRODUCTION

A gift to the human mind since the dawn of time has been the sense of wonder we feel at the sight of nature's more unusual or spectacular creations. Whenever on earth they have occurred in the past, or continue to prevail around us, these wonders have inspired great myths and legends to explain their seemingly mysterious origins and purpose. In Florida, such revelations of nature's splendor abound in the form of great crystalline rivers that rise from within the earth. In their unique profusion and resplendence, these springs have continued to fascinate us since primitive peoples first walked on to the peninsula more than 10,000 years ago.

Ancient cultures that first ventured into Florida long ago found primitive security in the plentiful food and campsites spring areas provided. In the mysteries of these upwelling waters their religions and legends were founded. Though little evidence remains of these early inhabitants, relics of their stone-age cultures and fossilized bones of their prey are found underwater among spring sands.

More than 2000 years ago, when most of the inhabitants of North America were tribes of nomadic hunter-gatherers, a settlement was established on Florida's gulf coast at the edge of a spring river. This colony, complete with an astronomical observatory, was surrounded by sufficient bounty that it prospered for 800 years. Then, at approximately the same period as the collapse of the Mayan culture that once flourished throughout Central America, the colony was abandoned. Along the banks of the Crystal River, remnants of this advanced civilization are preserved, including their enigmatic carved stone pillars, or "stelae," unlike any others known in the United States.

Ancient cultures' fascination with Florida's springs is perhaps best reflected in the early religions of primitive Florida's Paleo-Indians, who believed these springs held sacred waters with magical properties capable of curing their sick and healing their wounded. Indian nations of the region so revered their sacred waters that, even in times of war, they could meet at the edges of some springs in peace.

The first Spanish explorers in Florida were quick to believe that many kinds of treasures were to be found in this new and wondrous land. Influenced by native religions and rumors of sacred springs, legends were born of crystalline fountains of youth hidden deep in the interior of Florida. The arrival in Florida in 1513 of a Spanish officer named Ponce de León, and the mysterious expeditions he led throughout these regions, kindled the legends further. Though Ponce de León's search for a fountain of youth is more legend than fact, he is credited with the discovery of many springs during his probable mission of secretly searching for gold in Florida. Some springs still bear his name, and the legends of waters that heal and restore youth live on.

The now classic writings of colonial traveler and naturalist William Bartram in the 1770s did much to enhance the knowledge of Florida's springs and their inhabitants as well as of the flora and fauna of the primitive southeast. On commission from the king of England, William Bartram, with eyes tuned to the subtle nuances of this unknown and hazardous land, traversed a primal Florida, eloquently describing all he saw. Many of his original insights into the springs and their subterranean origins and realms remain accurate today.

The development of this region in the latter days of colonial America was influenced, in part, by the presence of springs. Their waters provided navigable rivers and streams, and, as their location and fame spread by word of mouth, civilization moved into the interior of Florida. Settlements were again founded on the banks of spring rivers or near headsprings, often at sites previously used by ancient cultures for thousands of years. A great many present-day Florida cities and towns are named after nearby springs.

The impressive clarity and size of Florida's springs have accounted for their greatest intrigue, but it was not until 1856, when Dr. Daniel G. Brinton visited Silver Springs, that the first scientific observations were made. Brinton was so moved by the environment of Silver Springs that he ranked it with Niagara Falls and the Mississippi River as one of the "grand hydrographical features of the North American continent." In 1859, Professor John LeConte described Silver Springs as "beautiful beyond description" and devised a number of experiments to measure the transparency of the spring's water. In one simple test, he discovered he could read the headline type of the New York

Herald while it was suspended 60 feet beneath the surface of the spring. Since these original investigations more than 100 years ago, the springs have attracted innumerable scientists in search of answers to the springs' many secrets, and those who study them now are no less intrigued than were Brinton and LeConte.

Today, the springs impart a considerable and growing contribution to the economy of Florida as well as providing recreation for millions of residents and tourists. A multitude of enterprises directly and indirectly influenced by springs are found in Florida. The larger springs in state parks, national forests and attractions that advertise underwater theater and glass-bottom boat rides are the most well known. Numerous dive resorts, fishing camps, canoe outfitters, restaurants, marinas, SCUBA shops, and campgrounds are present along springs and their rivers and streams. And health resorts established more than a century ago continue to attract visitors from around the world who come to bathe in spring waters still claimed to heal.

The peninsula of Florida contains one of the largest concentrations of freshwater springs in the world. More than 300 springs are known in the state, but, because they rise to the surface in forms and terrains so varied, many others likely flow uncounted, hidden in subtropical forest or wrapped in perimeters of cypress. Many springs are so small they barely trickle across a forest floor; others are the deepest and largest known springs in the world.

Springs also rise into the sea off Florida's shores in the shallow coastal waters of the Atlantic Ocean and Gulf of Mexico. Some submarine springs barely move grains of sand in ocean sediments, while others stream through cavernous openings to visibly disturb the surface of the sea with great intrusions of fresh water.

But, as remarkable as the springs are in their abundance and size, it is what lies beneath their mirrored surfaces that bestows their greatest fascination. There, hidden by depth and surface reflection, a freshwater kingdom exists unsurpassed in its beauty and abundance of life.

The many forms of springs, combined with their occurrence in the subtropical environment of Florida, have resulted in freshwater environments unparalleled in North America. There are more species of fishes, amphibians and reptiles in Florida than in any other comparable area of the world, and Florida's fresh waters are visited by more numbers of saltwater fishes than those of any other area of the United States. The springs play an important role in supporting this great profusion and diversity of life. Equally as important as the aquatic life the springs maintain are the other aquatic environments they affect and the varied terrestrial plant and animal life upon which the springs have influence.

Most springs, when they meet the surface of land, flow as rivers and streams that may wind for miles through live oak woods to finally meet and dilute the turbid flow of still other rivers. Other springs rise through river sediments or surface at river edges to form crystalline windows in otherwise dark waters. The springs are environments unto themselves, but they have mutual bonds with the environments through which they pass and into which they flow.

The springs constitute a varied and complex environment — one less known than most. By comparison, this environment is relatively small, but unlike most others, its realms extend far into regions where we cannot yet venture. Many people enjoy the shallow underwater areas with snorkel and mask; a few cave divers have explored some of the many subterranean caves using sophisticated gear; but deeper realms exist where no human has yet to penetrate.

The springs are in themselves an environment characterized by extreme contrasts. At their surface, exposed to the sun, there is brilliance, color, abundance of life. In their subterranean depths, there is eternal and sterile darkness. Divers have died in the exploration of these depths, but with each new person's discovery of these waters, a new sense of wonder and appreciation is born. There are few aquatic places in our world that rival the dimensions of splendor found in the springs of Florida.

These same springs that lured ancient peoples and caused civilizations to prosper, these sacred waters that kindled religion and reverence and spawned legends of eternal youth, and these same springs that inspired the gifted pen of Bartram are around us still. Indeed, as I write and as you read, they flow this moment to the sea.

Chapter 1

THE SPRINGS ENVIRONMENT

"Behold, for instance, a vast circular expanse before you, the waters of which are so extremely clear as to be absolutely diaphanous or transparent as the ether... But behold yet something far more admirable, see whole armies descending into an abyss, into the mouth of the bubbling fountain; they disappear! Are they gone forever? Is it real? I raise my eyes with terror and astonishment. I look down again to the fountain with anxiety, then behold them as it were emerging from the blue ether of another world. . . ."

William Bartram, 1775

The mouth of a subterranean river becomes the source of a surface stream where its water rushes through a vent in limestone bedrock. It flows with such force that it maintains a milky geyser of suspended sand and shells and forms a "boil" on the headspring surface.
Ichetucknee Springs State Park, Columbia County

The area that is now Florida was, in times before the dinosaur, part of a great plateau of weathered mountains that extended south from the main continental land mass of North America. This already ancient mountain range, or Floridan Plateau, sank slowly beneath the ocean, leaving in its wake a large and shallow sea surrounded by deep waters of the Gulf of Mexico and Atlantic Ocean.

The tropical sea that covered the plateau was ideally suited to a great abundance of marine life. Countless varieties of shellfish, coral and microscopic animals (foraminifera) flourished. As each organism died, its protective shell or covering of calcium and magnesium carbonates (limestone) remained, and each new generation grew upon the remnants of the old. Through ensuing ages, as new life evolved and diversified, as continents imperceptibly moved and changed form, the limestone thickened on the Floridan Plateau.

The gradual accumulation of limestone grew to such magnitude over thousands of centuries that, rather than reaching the surface to form reefs and islands, the limestone's massive weight forced the old plateau to settle still deeper into the earth. As sediments increased and the plateau settled further, the shallow sea environment continued for more millions of years.

Geologic forces within the earth's changing crust began to stress the sediments, warping them into a dome shape over the original rock plateau. In the recent geologic past, at a time when early humans first appeared on the planet, the limestone arched above the sea. A new land mass, resurrected from the sea, was formed again where it had not existed for millennia. This new peninsula was soon lush with tropical vegetation, and a vast array of creatures roamed its virgin terrain.

The porous limestone that composed the newborn peninsula was saturated with salt water in its final emergence from the sea. Fresh water, falling as tropical rain, was slowly absorbed by the limestone and floated upon the heavier salt water within the sediments. As more centuries passed, the continuous addition of fresh water gradually displaced the salt water downward into the lower regions of the limestone and, along the coasts, forced it laterally back into the sea.

Decaying vegetation mixed with the fresh water as it percolated into the ground, forming a mild carbonic acid solution. Combining with the already inherently soluble properties of limestone, the acidic water in a slow but persistent course dissolved a honeycomb of tunnels, fissures and caverns deep into the bedrock of Florida. The subterranean regions of Florida have thus become an immense rock sponge saturated with fresh water and meshed with underground rivers that flow through a complex maze of tunnels and passageways.

The limestone base formed in Florida's evolution extends in some regions to depths greater than 10,000 feet. This limestone now constitutes an underground reservoir, or "aquifer," enormous enough in size to store great volumes of fresh water. With constant resupply from rains, an overflow results and spills from the aquifer. These overflows, where they rise to the surface of the land, form the springs of Florida.

The springs of Florida are uniquely large and prolific because of the tremendous size of the aquifer that supports them. Two types of aquifers have the ability to create springs. Florida's springs are artesian springs, rising from an artesian aquifer that holds water confined beneath overlying impermeable material such as clay or nonporous bedrock.

Florida's limestone cap is exposed through spring waters at the source of the Crystal River, its many fractures clearly visible. Several springs emerge in this area to form a major manatee winter sanctuary and one of the most popular freshwater dive sites in the world for the opportunity it provides for underwater encounters with wild manatees. Crystal River, Citrus County

Artesian springs result when the hydrostatic or head pressure of water confined within the aquifer is sufficient to force water up through cracks and fissures in the overlying nonporous material. The height to which the pressure will force water is the potentiometric surface.

Artesian springs account for the largest springs in the world and respond to water conditions over a wide area within their aquifers. The amount of water an artesian spring produces remains fairly constant, and reactions to local water conditions are usually subtle.

In contrast, a nonartesian aquifer will exhibit springs where ground level has dipped below the

The porosity of Florida's limestone is visibly evident around these swimmers standing on the roof of an underwater cave. The exhaled air of divers in the cave below can percolate upwards through limestone bedrock as easily as rainwater can percolate down.
Ginnie Springs, Gilchrist County

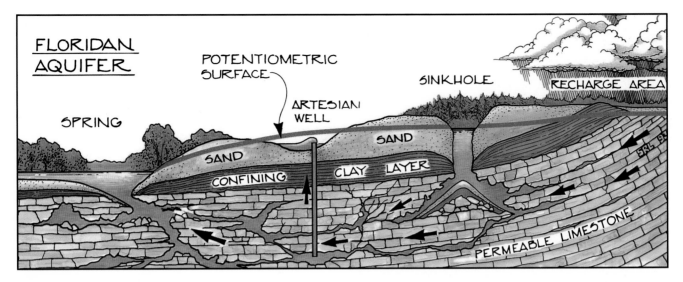

FLORIDAN AQUIFER

POTENTIOMETRIC SURFACE

ARTESIAN WELL

SPRING

SINKHOLE

RECHARGE AREA

SAND

SAND

CONFINING

CLAY LAYER

PERMEABLE LIMESTONE

surrounding water table. Water simply flows by gravity through porous ground or along cracks in nonporous rock to appear as a "seepage" spring in the lower area. Such springs are usually small and are the most common springs worldwide. The amount of water they produce is influenced directly by local water table conditions and rainfall.

Four major aquifers have been identified in Florida, but the Floridan Aquifer, located beneath the northern half of the state, is the most significant. The Floridan Aquifer is the only artesian aquifer in Florida, and from it flow the largest and greatest number of springs.

The greatest concentration of springs appears in north-central Florida, where the Floridan Aquifer is both near and at the surface of land and where rivers have eroded through confining beds of clay. Where the aquifer is deeper underground, there is sufficient pressure within it to force springs to the surface in other land areas more than 100 feet above sea level.

In many areas of Florida, a process continues where underground caves and shifting strata collapse to form sinks. Sinks that collapse into the aquifer will fill with water often having a slight lateral flow, but the water does not flow as a river or stream. Sinks can be likened to a hole in a soaked sponge.

In yet another form, a spring-siphon occurs, where a flowing underground stream rises to meet land's surface only to continue its course back underground rather than overland.

Water within the aquifer is replenished by rainfall where the limestone dome outcrops at the land's surface in north-central Florida and southern Alabama and Georgia — a massive recharge area estimated to encompass 13,000 square miles. The Floridan Aquifer has an equally massive capacity to store water. It is estimated that were the aquifer not present, Florida's annual 53 inches of rain could flood much of the state to a depth of several feet per year.

Aside from being the source of Florida's springs, the Floridan Aquifer is one of the state's most important and valuable natural resources. The aquifer is the source of municipal water supplies for such major metropolitan areas as Tallahassee, Gainesville, Jacksonville, Ocala, Orlando, Cape Canaveral, and Tampa-St. Petersburg. In addition, it provides water to tens of thousands of domestic, industrial and irrigational wells throughout the northern half of the state. The demand for water stored in the aquifer reaches billions of gallons per day. But natural flow from the aquifer in the form of springs is more than three times greater than all of civilization's uses combined.

A number of factors have combined in Florida to make this karst terrain (soluble limestone and sinkholes) one of the most favorable

The clearer flow of a headspring is still visible through turbid floodwaters of a nearby stream flowing over Ponce de Leon Spring. If floodwaters rise sufficiently high, the spring will reverse flow causing the floodwaters to "siphon" down into the aquifer.
Ponce de Leon State Recreation Area, Holmes County

regions in the world for the formation of springs. Warm climate, heavy rainfall, prolific decaying vegetation, high humidity and limestone rock thousands of feet thick have left Florida with its legacy of springs and spring-fed rivers. Because each of these factors played a varying role in the creation of each spring, every spring is unique in its rate of flow, size and design.

Springs are classified into categories according to the volume of water they produce in a given amount of time. Their flow rates are averages of several measurements described in terms of cubic feet per second (ft^3/sec) or million gallons per day (mgd).

The largest springs are classified first-magnitude springs, in which flow rates meet or exceed 100 ft^3/sec or 64.6 mgd. Seventy-five first-magnitude springs are known to exist in the United States. Florida has more than one-third of these with 27 first-magnitude springs having a combined flow rate of over six billion gallons per day. The smaller second-magnitude springs have an average flow rate between 10 and 100 ft^3/sec and account for about 70 of Florida's springs. Approximately 190 springs are third-magnitude springs. Each of these produces less than 10 ft^3/sec or 6.46 mgd.

Although second- and third-magnitude springs comprise more than 250 of Florida's known 300 springs, their flow rates account for only one-fourth of total spring flow. The greatest amount of spring water originates from the tremendous flows of first-magnitude springs. A complete world inventory of springs and flow rates is not available, but Florida's 27 first-magnitude springs alone are believed to

exceed, in volume of water discharged, those springs in all countries of the world.

The amount of water a spring provides is never constant over a long term, but neither does it vary to a great degree. The annual rainfall over the aquifer is the primary factor affecting flow rates. Seasonal variations in flow rate occur with increased flow in the fall resulting from the heavy rains of summer. Because of its great size, the aquifer shows a lag time in returning that rainwater as spring discharge. So vast is the aquifer, spring water emerging from it may be hundreds of years old.

Most springs show little effect from localized, short-term rainfall. But some springs, with underground access to nearby surface streams, will increase their flow following heavy rains, discharging dark, tannic water from the nearby river. Others may spew white, cloudy water thought to result from the precipitation of dissolved limestone following rapid pressure or temperature changes when discharged.

Springs located near rivers may on occasion be inundated during flood periods of the river. If the head pressure of the water above the spring exceeds that within the aquifer, the spring will reverse its flow, creating a "siphon" into the aquifer. When the river recedes, the spring will again reverse itself and flow normally.

Springs are generally thought of in terms of cold water, but Florida's springs issue waters surprisingly warm. On the average, the waters of Florida's northern springs vary in temperature from 66^0 to 75^0F, and southern springs range from 75^0 to 87^0F. Because temperatures are largely determined by the depth of a spring's source within the aquifer, any given spring's temperature remains fairly constant. Springs with the deepest origins will have the warmest waters.

Studies made at Silver Springs have found that the main headspring has more than one underground source. Silver Springs rises to the land surface at the confluence of five subterranean rivers, each arriving from a different direction. Water temperature of rivers moving from the northwest varies from 67^0 to 68^0F, while rivers arriving from the southeast are almost 10^0 warmer, ranging from 75^0 to 76^0F. The confluence of these five rivers gives the main spring a constant temperature of 72^0F.

The waters of Florida's springs are world-famous for their clarity and purity, but all spring waters contain a number of dissolved minerals, most of which are invisible and undetectable except by

chemical analysis. Spring waters in Florida are distinctly moderately hard with a relatively high dissolved content of calcium and magnesium carbonates obtained in the water's passage through limestone. Many spring waters contain concentrations of dissolved salt acquired from the spring's source mixing with seawater or passing through deposits of salt residue remaining from the aquifer's origin in the sea. Other springs are noted for their green coloration and odor resulting from a high content of sulphur in their waters. Whatever a spring's quality of water, it typically reflects the mineral contents of sediments that line its course to the surface.

Some coastal springs rest in a delicate balance of providing fresh water or being contaminated with high concentrations of seawater. If human demand on fresh water becomes too great, or natural depletion of fresh water occurs in border regions of the aquifer, salt water may move into spring systems. Saltwater intrusions have in the past required the development of new well locations and alternate sources of water for municipalities. A spring's

As water rises through and blows sand from the bottom of a headspring pool, it enters a world brilliant with sunlight, lush with the green of vegetation and teeming with aquatic life. The underwater landscapes of springs take on many forms ranging from small sand depressions a few yards wide to immense current-filled basins hued in blue and rimmed with cliffs of sculptured limestone and swaying plants.
Rainbow Springs State Park, Marion County

freshwater environment is also threatened if saltwater levels reach toxic proportions.

The subterranean domain of Florida is a large and complex facet of the spring environment. Its hidden realms run deep and span thousands of cubic miles. The multitude of events occurring within these limestone depths provide remarkable environments both beneath and at the surface of Florida's springs.

Spring waters are uniquely alive, and visible life is remarkable in its abundance and contrast. In these waters live one of the largest of all reptiles, the smallest of North American freshwater fishes, the largest of freshwater snails in the United States, the migratory manatee and transient saltwater fishes from the sea. Spring waters are filled with constant movement and color — schools of fish glide by reflecting sunlight into glittering flashes, turtles bob to the surface, and plants bend and bow, pointing the way downstream.

It is an impressive world. In few other freshwater communities are the residents so visible in their fascinating routines or their habitat and niches so

obvious and understood. Spring inhabitants have a rare opportunity to display their array of bright colors normally camouflaged by the deep browns and greens they attain in darker or more turbid waters.

And in few other aquatic worlds are the inhabitants at such apparent ease as they pass by the nose of their predators. As nature intends, the conflicts for survival are prevalent here, but in this crystalline environment there is less an element of surprise. The ancient and firm rule prevails here: that the sick, the weak and the old are taken first so that the best of their species will spawn the next generations. This is, except for brief moments of struggle, a serene and soundless place.

The luxuriant vegetation that characterizes larger springs is an invaluable part of the springs environment. In its tremendous profusion it is the mainstay of the springs, keeping headspring shores and banks free of erosion, providing countless niches and cover for spring inhabitants, furnishing food for others, and adding necessary oxygen to the water. This infusion of oxygen into the water can be of such magnitude that on sunny days the billions of tiny bubbles rising to the surface from the leaves of plants will visibly haze the transparency of the water. The plants are the major foundations upon which all animal life depends in spring waters, but it is the transparency of the water itself that is the foundation for the abundance of all life in this environment.

The transparency of water largely determines the amount of the sun's energy that will penetrate it and be harnessed by aquatic plants, algae and the microscopic plants — phytoplankton. Plants utilize the free energy of sunlight to photosynthesize their food and maintain life. Because sunlight penetrates deeply into the clear and warm waters of the springs, plant life flourishes.

As spring water leaves its source, it creates a stream environment often more lush in vegetation and with more variation in inhabitants than headsprings. The eel grass (*Vallisneria neotropicalis*) that lines this stream's course is the most common plant of the springs flowing environment.
Ichetucknee Springs State Park, Columbia County

The remarkable clarity of Florida's spring waters is also responsible for the blue hue distinctive of deeper springs. This blue color, similar to that of a clear sky, results from clear water filtering the sunlight, leaving visible only the blue wavelength of the spectrum.

In addition to the profusion of visible plant life, there is an almost invisible but equally vital growth of algae and phytoplankton. Of all plants in the springs, these seemingly insignificant forms contribute most in the generation of the springs' abundant animal life. These algae, in their immense numbers, capture the sun's energy, maintain it in their living cells, and ultimately give that energy to other and higher forms of spring creatures.

There are at least 25 species of algae and phytoplankton known to occur in the springs environment. Most of these are diatoms, one-celled microscopic plants encased in glasslike shells of silica, each with a unique shell design and pattern. Although diatoms and many forms of algae are invisible to the naked eye, some forms are quite apparent as they thrive in the springs environment.

There is little in the springs that is not covered with some form of algae growth. Virtually all objects, plants, sticks and limestone walls that are exposed to the sun or receive reflected light from bright sand bottoms have a layer of algae. Some forms of algae grow only in deeper depths, adding a pink shade to limestone walls; others grow only on the shells of turtles; some form brown or green films on logs and plant leaves; yet others, like *Spirogyra* and *Cladophera*, are easily identified as their bright green clumps of hairlike filaments hang downstream, slowly undulating in the current. Often, during the high sun of midday, clumps of these algae are carried to the surface by the great numbers of oxygen bubbles they produce and that become caught in the algae strands.

The vascular, or leaved, plants such as eel grass are as numerous in species as algae and diatoms, but they are limited by the pressures of the water's depth to spring terrains less than 25 feet deep. The algae and diatoms, on the other hand, flourish throughout the springs environment as deep as light will penetrate. The vascular plants, in addition to their own contribution, provide an immense amount of surface area for the foundation of algal growth. Each species of plant has its place and function, and together they are the basis for the diversity and abundance of animal life that characterizes Florida's springs as one of the richest freshwater environments in the world.

Snails constitute a first visible step in the process by which plants support the animals inhabiting the springs. With a great profusion of plant and algae life, there is a similar profusion of snails that depend upon the plants. These snails in turn support a profusion of fishes that feed upon the snails. Upon these smaller fishes fall the larger predator fishes. A chain of life exists here, each link depending upon the next, and the last still depending upon the first.

Impressed by the extraordinary richness of the springs environment, scientists have conducted revealing studies at Silver Springs to measure the role played by algal and vascular plant life in supporting the abundant community of spring creatures. In measuring this productivity, the researchers began at the very base of the food chain with the algae and vegetation. They discovered that in the course of a year the production by weight of algae and vegetation alone was 12.85 pounds per square yard — a productivity greater than that of many cultivated crops.

The springs environment is a fertile and bountiful place, an actuality most visibly reflected in the myriad profusion of its many realms and various creatures. Inhabitants occupy all of its regions. Some huddle at the water's surface, while others glide through its open expanses; some hide in dark shadows of vegetation and beneath the sands. Some avoid the light of day and emerge only at night. And there are others with no need of eyes that inhabit even its deep subterranean source in the complete absence of light. It is a magnificent and rare environment, as are many of the creatures that inhabit it.

As a river snail grazes upon a layer of algae covering the leaves of red primrose, it converts plant matter to animal matter. Their algae food plentiful, river snails inhabit the springs environment in tremendous profusion. Cypress Springs, Washington County

CHAPTER 2

Springs inhabitants

"At the same instant innumerable bands of fish are seen, some clothed in the most brilliant colors; the voracious crocodile stretched along at full length, as the great trunk of a tree in size, the devouring garfish, inimical trout, and all the varieties of gilded painted bream, the barbed catfish,dreaded sting-ray, skate and flounder, spotted bass, sheepshead and ominous drum; all in their separate bands and communities, with free and unsuspicious intercourse performing their evolutions...It is amazing and almost incredible, what troops and bands of fish, and other watery inhabitants are now in sight, all peaceable, and in what variety of gay colors and forms, continually ascending and descending, roving, and figuring amongst one another, yet every tribe associating separately. . . ."

William Bartram, 1775

Attracted to the likely offering of bread from a glass-bottom boat nearby, a variety of spring fishes congregate in the large headspring pool of Silver Springs.
Silver Springs, Marion County

Alligator
An unmistakable creature stands at ease, posed like a dinosaur. An alligator, the largest reptile of North America, reveals at night a rarely seen underwater view of a resting stance, in this instance, stretching on its toes to reach the surface. From above, only its nostrils and eyes will appear on the water. From below, its startling, obvious form is not likely to escape notice.
(Also called American alligator)
Alexander Springs, Ocala National Forest

Bluegill
Noted for their tendency to hover beneath boats and docks, these bluegills are members of the bream family most often seen in Florida's central and southern springs. Easily identified by their dark vertical bars, these are a distinct Florida subspecies of the more common northern bluegill.
(Also called bluegill sunfish, bluegill bream)
Rainbow River, Marion County

Apple Snail
Seeming more like an unknown denizen of the deep than a harmless and common springs inhabitant, this apple snail feeds by night atop a sunken log where its spring joins the turbid waters of the St. Johns River. Apple snails, some of which reach over three inches in diameter, are the largest snails inhabiting fresh waters of the United States. Found only in Florida and southern Georgia, they are virtually the only food of two Florida birds: the limpkin and the endangered Everglades kite (snail hawk). Apple snails are responsible for the curious masses of light pink, pea-sized eggs found just above the water around Florida's lakes, rivers and springs.
Blue Springs State Park, Volusia County

Blackbanded Darter
A darter common to Florida's springs, the blackbanded darter is easily distinguishable by its large size (it may reach five inches) and black blotches running along its sides. Preferring swift waters, blackbanded darters are often found in great numbers resting on open sands or atop sunken logs in spring runs.
Cypress Springs, Washington County

Blue Tilapia
Far from their native Africa, these blue tilapia are unwelcome invaders of some Florida springs. Through an accidental introduction, they have become one of Florida's most undesirable exotics, overwhelming native species for food, space and spawning sites.
Silver Glen Springs, Ocala National Forest

Bowfin
A bowfin displays its ancient bulletlike form as it moves from shaded cover beneath a dock. More abundant in turbid waters, spring runs that flow into major rivers often have a great abundance of bowfins where spring and river meet. Like the gars, they must occasionally go to the surface for a gulp of air.
(Also called mudfish, dogfish, grindel)
Manatee Springs State Park, Levy County

SPRINGS INHABITANTS

Brown Darter
A two-inch female brown darter, hidden among penny-
wort and snails, lives on springs bottoms
in a small tropical world. Both the female and
the red-spotted male are among the bravest of springs
fishes. A patient diver will find darters
sitting on an outstretched hand or camera.
Ichetucknee Springs State Park, Columbia County

Chain Pickerel
Disturbed from its lair in vegetated shadows, a chain
pickerel exposes its golden coloration as it moves into
sunlit waters. These are solitary fishes that prefer to hide
motionless and unseen among vegetation where their
green and yellow markings blend perfectly underwater
with plants and ripples of sunlight.
(Also called mud pickerel, grass pickerel, chain pike)
Morrison Springs, Walton County

Black Crappie
Two crappies hang gracefully in formation at the edge
of a limestone cliff. Not an abundant spring resident,
it is, however, a prolific, sought-after gamefish in
lakes throughout Florida and one of the
state's most attractive native fishes.
(Also called crappie, speckled perch)
Blue Springs, Gilchrist County

Flier
Backdropped by trees and sky, a group of fliers hangs in the headspring crevasse of Otter Springs, the only spring in Florida where they were found by the author and where that day they were the only fish present. Similar in size to bluegills and identifiable by their round profile and characteristic horizontal rows of black spots across their sides, fliers are more likely to be found in darker, tannic waters as in the nearby Suwannee River.
(Also called millpond flier, round sunfish)
Otter Springs, Gilchrist County

Florida Softshell Turtle
Displaying its webbed feet and gliding form that make it one of the largest and swiftest of spring turtles in water or on land, a Florida softshell patrols the edge of its domain. Not often so easily approached, it spends much of its time hiding among vegetation or buried in sand with only its head protruding. Ordinarily a shy creature, a softshell when hidden feels disguised enough to be handled, petted, and even have its snout rubbed by divers.
(Also called leatherback)
Alexander Springs, Ocala National Forest

Florida Gar
With white teeth exposed, the predatory Florida gar glides
through sunlit shallows where its spring joins the
Suwannee River. The Florida gar is a close relative of the
longnose gar but lacks the long, beaklike mouth and size
of the longnose. Primarily river inhabitants, they exhibit
appreciable populations only in larger springs and rivers.
(Also called spotted gar, short-nose gar, billfish)
Manatee Springs State Park, Levy County

Florida Snapping Turtle
In transit at night across a deep spring basin, a turtle uncommon to springs brakes in a momentary encounter before calmly continuing on its dark foray. More abundant in the Everglades, the Florida variety of snapping turtle is among the largest of freshwater turtles. Characterized by its large head, saw-toothed tail, powerful jaws and vile temper if approached on land, in water the snapper is a relatively timid creature.
(Also called snapper)
Alexander Springs, Ocala National Forest

Freshwater Shrimp
Translucent in dark waters at night, a freshwater shrimp makes its way across the open waters of a spring. Rarely exceeding one inch in size, the freshwater variety of shrimp closely resembles the much larger saltwater species. Freshwater shrimp abound by the thousands in springs with abundant vegetation. Their presence is likely to go unheeded except at night when, if exposed to light, large concentrations are visible as their eyes glow brilliant red.
(Also called freshwater prawn)
Naked Spring, Gilchrist County

Golden Shiner
One of the colorful spectacles of the springs environment is the underwater swim-by of golden shiner schools. As they slide through glasslike waters, they catch and reflect sunlight into waves and shimmers of golden flashes. Shiners are present throughout Florida fresh waters, but in springs they primarily inhabit the larger, deeper springs and spring rivers. Larger wild shiners are a preferred bait for trophy largemouth bass.
(Also called Florida shiner, wild shiner)
Alexander Springs, Ocala National Forest

Greater Siren
One of the more startling moments to a canoer or
spring diver, and one of the most difficult to
photograph, is that of a sudden and close encounter
with a greater siren rising quickly to the surface. After
a momentary surface visit for two or three quick gulps
of air, a siren will dart quickly down and return to its
dark cover. Commonly mistaken for eels when sighted
from the surface, sirens are among the largest of
amphibians, some exceeding three feet in length.
Manatee Springs State Park, Levy County

Lake Chubsucker
Against a green background of potamogeton and flanked
by rising stems of coontail, a pair of chubsuckers glides
through crystalline waters. In contrast to their indelicate
name, the chubsuckers are especially graceful fishes,
coasting and darting in spurts. They swim as if flying,
avoiding obstacles with artful precision.
Rainbow River, Marion County

Largemouth Bass
Seeking shade beneath a dock among their many prey, two Florida largemouth bass exhibit the form and authority that have given them their name and made them famous as one of the most respected and sought-after gamefish of North America. A subspecies of the more common northern largemouth, the native Florida largemouth occurs naturally only in peninsular Florida.
(Also called black bass, green bass, green trout)
Blue Springs, Gilchrist County

Least Killifish
Prowling the surface along the bark of a cypress tree, a least killifish betrays its tiny size as it approaches a river snail. A noteworthy inhabitant of the springs environment, least killifish are the smallest vertebrate animals in North America. Less than an inch in length and well blended into their environment, they exist throughout the fresh waters of Florida in abundance and obscurity.
Peacock Springs State Recreation Area, Suwannee County

Loggerhead Musk Turtle
A loggerhead musk turtle peers from an algae-laden ledge 15 feet underwater. A subspecies almost endemic to Florida springs, these negatively buoyant turtles roam spring bottoms, never having to reach the surface for air. Their ability to absorb oxygen through their skin finds them occasionally in underwater caves where no other turtle would normally venture. Often misidentified as small snapping turtles, loggerheads reach a maximum size of only five inches.
(Also called loggerhead)
Blue Springs, Gilchrist County

Longnose Gar
Leaving a large congregation of its companions near the surface, a longnose gar descends to make a close inspection pass near divers rarely seen in this spring. Commonly mistaken for alligator gars found only in the western panhandle, longnose gars are often seen rolling at the surface for periodic gulps of air. Living relics of an ancient order of fishes, they will drown if unable to reach the surface.
(Also called garpike, billfish, northern mailed fish, needlenose)
Wakulla Springs State Park, Wakulla County

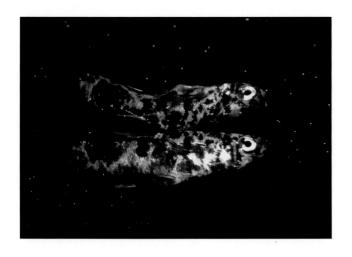

Mosquitofish
Its image mirrored just under the water's surface, a one-inch male mosquitofish, resplendent in coloration, searches for food. Their fondness for mosquito larvae has led to their introduction into many areas as a natural agent in mosquito control.
Alexander Springs, Ocala National Forest

Redear Sunfish
Secure in numbers among corridors of available space, the largest and most timid of Florida's bream species uncharacteristically hold their ground. Voracious predators of snails, redears well deserve their common name — "shellcrackers." The crunching sound of their feeding is audible to divers if in close proximity.
(Also called shellcracker, redeared bream)
Crystal Springs, Pasco County

Redbreast Sunfish
The redbreast sunfish is one of the most colorful of the Florida sunfishes and, among divers and snorkelers, among the most amiable of spring creatures. They are easily fed by hand, often allowing themselves to be touched or brushed aside.
(Also called yellowbelly bream, redbelly, river bream)
Rainbow River, Marion County

Redeye Chub
Staying close to their protective cover, a school of redeye chubs weaves skillfully through vegetation lining their spring habitat. A nomadic species that constantly roams open springs basins, they are also reported by cave explorers to be one of few fishes to penetrate deeply into spring cave systems. These small fishes, often misidentified as a released aquarium species, are the most common schooling native species of the springs and rarely are found outside spring habitats.
Ichetucknee Springs State Park, Columbia County

Sailfin Molly
In the tranquil backwaters of a spring run, a male sailfin molly, surrounded by his harem, defends his territory against an intruder in a flamboyant display of breeding behavior. The male's striking appearance and ability to erect his dorsal "sailfin" attract receptive females to mate and permit him to appear more formidable when dueling with competing males.
Ichetucknee Springs State Park, Columbia County
Photo by Tim Whitney

Spotted Sucker
A spotted sucker, discovered in its nightly rounds, feeds heartily on the small invertebrates and snails it takes from the sands. Not often seen during the day, by night they enter spring runs from rivers or emerge from their cover to roam springs in search of food.
(Also called striped sucker, black sucker)
Blue Springs, Gilchrist County

Spring Crayfish
Defiant and armed with muscular claws, a spring crayfish approached at night prepares to defend its cave in the algae-coated cliff of a limestone wall. In springs where their populations are high, they can be seen at night in great numbers, each standing watch from a similar niche or burrow. One of the most colorful species in North America, these crayfish are only found in the springs and spring-fed river systems of northern Florida.
(Also called crawfish, crab)
Blue Springs, Gilchrist County

Spotted Sunfish
Displaying the distinctive turquoise of the lower eye and the spots that give it its common name, a member of a spotted sunfish aggregation exhibits well the large pectoral and pelvic fins that make these members of the sunfish family notably maneuverable fishes. An abundant spring species, they are most common in deep holes of runs and in deeper waters of headsprings.
(Also called stumpknocker, spotted bream)
Blue Springs, Gilchrist County

Stinkpot Turtle
Easily approached underwater at night, a stinkpot turtle is captured close up. A member of the musk turtle family, the stinkpot is especially capable of secreting the reasons for its common name if mishandled. Should a turtle ever fall on your head or drop in your canoe, it most likely will be a stinkpot. Though seldom found out of water, they will inexplicably climb trees to record heights in the world of turtles. Sleeping in the sun, they usually do not awake until you pass beneath, and then, startled, they fall from their lofty perches.
(Also called stinking jim, skillpot)
Rainbow River, Marion County

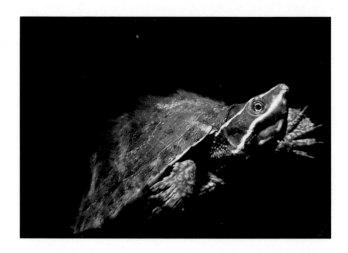

Suwannee Bass
Maintaining its position and territory in the current of a spring river, a defiant Suwannee bass observes the camera and photographer as they drift by. These bass are rare creatures in the world of fresh water. Though close relatives of the largemouth bass, the Suwannee bass are endemic to northern Florida and southern Georgia where they inhabit only the Suwannee and Ochlockonee rivers and their tributaries.
(Also called black bass, green trout, southern small mouth)
Ichetucknee Springs State Park, Columbia County

Suwannee Cooter
A young Suwanee cooter in rapid transit, a member of perhaps the swiftest turtle species in the United States, is most often visible sunning in large groups on logs and banks. They are inclined to wander by land and sea, and their empty shells have been found far from water; some have turned up in Havana markets as part of the catch of Cuban trawlers.
(Also called Suwannee chicken, slider)
Blue Springs, Gilchrist County

Tadpole Madtom
The secretive tadpole madtom is a springs inhabitant rarely seen except by fossil-hunting divers. Hidden beneath rocks and debris, the two-inch madtom is abundant in Florida's springs and rivers, but its nocturnal nature makes it almost unknown. Like other members of the catfish family, it is equipped with sharp, venomous spines hidden in its pectoral and dorsal fins. A sting from a madtom is especially painful.
Rainbow River, Marion County

CHAPTER 3

THE CAVES

"...where those who are so fortunate as to effect a retreat into the conductor, and escape the devouring jaws of the fearful alligator and armed gar, descend into the earth, through the wells and cavities or vast perforations of the rocks, and from thence are conducted and carried away, by secret subterranean conduits and gloomy vaults, to other distant lakes and rivers; and it does not appear improbable, but that in some future day this vast savanna or lake of waters, in the winter season will be discovered to be in great measure filled with its finny inhabitants, who are strangers or adventurers, from other lakes, ponds, and rivers, by subterraneous rivulets and communications to this rocky, dark door or outlet, whence they ascend to its surface, spread over and people the winter lake, where they breed, increase and continue as long as it is underwater, or during pleasure, for they are at all seasons to be seen ascending and descending through the rocks. . . ."

William Bartram, 1775

Descending to deep realms of an aquifier cloaked in eternal and total darkness, passageways twist and branch to confuse human explorers here. Forbidding to most of us, this seemingly sterile maze provides unique habitats to an array of spring life and remains one of the last unexplored regions of Florida.
Morrison Springs, Walton County

Beneath the sunlit environment of the springs there exists another environment in marked contrast to that on the surface. The environment of subterranean caves and tunnels does not teem with the activity of life. The only visible movements are occasional wisps of sand shifting with the force of unseen currents. The only colors are solitary shades of white and brown. And throughout its realms, except in twilight areas near its access to the surface, it is an environment cloaked in a form of black darkness found only with the complete and total absence of light.

Like the surface above, the underground world takes on many forms. Some springs rise from tunnels so circular that they appear to be man-made vertical shafts. Others are twisting, turning, ever-tightening spirals that descend randomly to extreme depth. And yet others weave deep into the limestone, rise to the surface as crystalline pools, and descend again.

Though this domain seems forbidding and sterile, there are, nevertheless, creatures inhabiting these stark regions of winding corridors and caverns. Of those few, most are nocturnal fishes that retreat to these dark niches to avoid the light of day. At dusk they venture from underground to roam the open expanses of the surface environment. At dawn they will return. Others have completely adapted to this extreme environment of depth and darkness and never leave it.

Cave Diver
Against strong currents of first-magnitude flow and through tangles of downed trees, a diver makes his way down the eye-shaped shaft at Blue Springs State Park. At 120 feet down, the tunnel becomes too small for further passage. Only certified cave divers are allowed past a warning sign at 50-foot depth where, in the darkness below, an invisible sideways intrusion of clear water blows with considerable force. Termed "the hydrant," it has blown masks off divers' faces and regulators from their mouths.
Blue Springs State Park, Volusia County
Photo by Tim Whitney

American Eel
At 90-foot depths and more than 100 feet inside a cavern room, American eels flee in every direction from bright underwater lights. Hundreds of eels populate this cave near a large panhandle river. Eels are the farthest habitual penetrators of submerged cave systems in Florida, often observed by cave explorers thousands of feet inside spring caves.
(Also called Atlantic eel, freshwater eel, silver eel)
Morrison Springs, Walton County

Albino Cave Crayfish
In striking contrast to the colors of limestone and fossilized shells, a troglobitic crayfish almost 100 feet underwater reveals its adaptations to the harsh demands of the cave environment. The absence of light requires no coloration and, though eye stalks are present, eyes never develop. The disturbance caused by a diver's presence in a cave evidently attracts these blind creatures. A cave that at first appearance may show no signs of their presence will often, after a few moments, reveal crayfish emerging from cracks and crevices to surround the intruder.
(Also called troglobitic crayfish, cave crayfish)
Big Blue Springs, Wacissa River, Jefferson County

Southern Brown Bullhead
One of the most abundant cave fishes are the brown bullheads or "butter cats." This group, encountered at night outside their cave, show tattered fins and wounds from fighting swift currents among their abrasive limestone niches. Large panhandle springs have especially large populations of brown bullheads, often inhabiting a cave system with a number of large groups, each group claiming a separate region of the cave.
(Also called butter cat, bullhead)
Silver Glen Spring, Ocala National Forest

For those divers who venture here, the cave environment is a fascinating, compelling place. Infinite forms and abstractions of sculptured limestone line its corridors, in places worn smooth by the ever-present impress of moving water throughout the millennia. Tunnels that appear to tighten to small apertures suddenly open to reveal immense rooms leading to a maze of more corridors. In other passageways, fossil shells, shapes and bones of creatures from ancient seas protrude from walls, floors and ceilings as reminders of the origins of this captivating and hidden world.

There is no visual sense of water being present here. It is so perfectly clear. It entices one to forget.

The often-present drag of invisible currents can be the only reminder, in some places pushing gently, and elsewhere suddenly slamming an unsuspecting diver against a limestone wall. This environment pulls, attracts, asking to be explored, to reveal what new wonders may be around its many corners. But visitors here should well pay heed to the legacy of many of these caves. To the untrained or careless, this is an environment as dangerous as it is beautiful.

With proper training and equipment, diving and exploring Florida's subterranean cave systems can be an exciting and safe adventure. Thousands of divers each year enter this intriguing world without dangerous incident. But for some who ventured

Fossil Bones
Florida's Ice Age history as a haven for mega-fauna characteristic of the Pleistocene can be found in the fossil record of giant sloths, camels and great bears preserved in spring caves. Among the many vestiges are these fossil leg bones of a mastodon. Originally discovered within Wakulla's immense cave almost 200 feet underwater, these bones were moved to the cave entrance to be visible from the surface.
Wakulla Springs State Park, Wakulla County

Shadow Bass
The distant reaches of a spring cave reveal unlikely residents, their cave entrance visible far in the background at a depth of 50 feet. Shadow bass, a rare spring inhabitant, occur only in Florida west of the panhandle's Apalachicola River. Their preference of a deep cave habitat over open water terrain is unexplainable. At depths over 80 feet, far from ambient light, other bass in this cave can be found hovering vertically at cave ceilings, nose up and against trapped bubbles of divers' exhalations, possibly obtaining oxygen in waters otherwise low in its content. (Also called rock bass)
Vortex Spring, Holmes County

Spotted Bullhead
Rarely seen except at night, this spotted bullhead displays the tattered fins of a strong current cave dweller. It is so gorged from its night feeding venture that it prefers to perch atop a boulder than to attempt its usual success at fleeing the lights of a night diver.
(Also called spotted catfish, speckled cat, snail cat)
Blue Springs, Gilchrist County

A powerful current blows hair and exhaled bubbles sideways in Ginnie Springs cavern where an iron grate at 55-foot depth prevents further access to an extensive cave system that has killed 27 divers. Once responsible for the loss of many divers, the spring is now one of Florida's safest and more spectacular cavern dives.
Ginnie Springs, Gilchrist County

here unprepared, to dive here has meant their death. Since the first Florida cave dive occurred in Blue Springs (Jug Hole) along the Ichetucknee River in 1951, more than 300 divers have died in these cave systems. In recent years, through the efforts of cave diving training organizations and the development of new techniques and equipment, cave diving fatalities are becoming a less frequent tragedy. But unfortunately they still occur.

Research into cave diving accidents has revealed an unfortunate pattern in the reasons why divers, often in groups of two, three or four at a time, die in these caves. In most instances, divers simply, but tragically, became lost in a cave system maze, ran out of air and drowned. Some divers

inadvertently stirred up silt, becoming lost in water where visibility that was hundreds of feet suddenly became zero. Other divers penetrated caves too far and ran out of air before they could return to the entrance.

Any diver who wishes to see these intriguing realms should first be properly trained and certified for cave diving. It is an emotionally and physically demanding, equipment-oriented undertaking and not for everyone. Do not venture here if you are not thoroughly prepared. It is an environment too unforgiving where the smallest infraction of the rules can cost you your life. (See Appendix B for more about safe cave diving.)

White Catfish
One of the world's largest and most protected springs reveals a large school of white catfish almost 100 feet underwater in the source of the Wakulla River. Often found deep into cave systems, white catfish are one of the most common catfish in springs with subterranean access, but individuals of this size in such large, organized schools are rare.
Wakulla Springs State Park, Wakulla County

Cave explorer Dustin Clesi inspects a diver's warning sign he placed at 60-foot depth where all surface light disappears in this cave. A cave diving instructor and team member of record cave explorations, Clesi is occasionally called upon to recover bodies of divers who ignore these signs.
Little River Spring, Suwannee County

THE CAVES

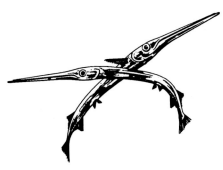

CHAPTER 4

The Saltwater Visitors

"Now they come forward rapidly, and instantly emerge, with the elastic expanding column of crystalline waters, into the circular basin or funnel; see how gently they rise, some upright, others obliquely, or seem to lay as it were on their sides, suffering themselves to be gently lifted or borne up, by the expanding fluid towards the surface, sailing or floating like butterflies in the cerulean ether: then again they as gently descend, diverge and move off; when they rally, form again and rejoin their kindred tribes."

William Bartram, 1775

Having just traveled seven miles up the Crystal River from the Gulf of Mexico, some members of a large school of gray snappers hover in the headspring pool of King's Spring while others turn into the current and descend into a large cave below. This spring where ocean and fresh water meet is one of the most fascinating and educational springs in Florida. King's Spring, Crystal River National Wildlife Refuge

What at first may appear to be the scene of an ocean reef in the preceding photo is in actuality a fascinating spectacle of transition in the springs environment. Hundreds of oceanic snappers backed by thousands of oceanic mullet force aside smaller freshwater fishes. In those springs with close access to the sea, the worlds of fresh water and ocean meet to reveal a wondrous array of inhabitants. Bluegills and bass swim with tarpon and shark, golden shiners dodge the darting, twisting attack of school-ing jacks, and gray snappers shed their schooling markings, descend into caves —a habitat not unlike the wrecks and coral crevices they prefer in the sea — and share their niches with white catfish and eels. The springs environment, active with the presence of visitors from the sea, is a spectacle of color, competition and complexity.

Large west coast springs and spring rivers mark the northernmost winter range of Florida's most well-known marine mammal, the manatees, that migrate yearly from cooling winter oceans for refuge in warm spring sanctuaries. Inland springs that flow ultimately to the sea shelter juvenile flounder camouflaged in white sands and vegetation on headspring slopes. American shad enter the mouth of the St. Johns River, travel a hundred miles up-stream to the Oklawaha River and then to the Silver River, emerging finally in the brilliant clarity of Silver Springs. After spawning, their arduous journey of almost 200 miles is immediately traversed again downstream. Mullet in winding schools, and needle-fish skimming the surface in small groups, weave through hundreds of headspring pools after a yet further journey, both species ubiquitous nomads of Florida rivers and springs.

That freshwater environments are visited by fishes innately marine is not, in itself, an unusual event; it occurs at the edges of continents world-wide. But in Florida, more saltwater fishes enter fresh water than in any other area of the United States.

In Florida waters, both marine and fresh, more than 1,100 species of fish are known to occur. Most are marine. Their numbers represent approximately one-fourth of all fish species known in the entire northern portion of the western hemisphere. That a great many oceanic fishes are entering Florida's fresh water is accordingly no coincidence. The tremendous length of Florida's coastline and the profusion of springs and spring-fed rivers along it that flow to the Atlantic and Gulf provide oceanic species with a great number of avenues of entry with easy access for many fishes to interior regions of the state. The greatest numbers and variety of marine species can be seen in winter when springs are warmer than surrounding oceanic waters.

The appearance of the gray snapper school pictured here descending to enter a cave entrance is an uncommon sight in the overall springs environ-ment. Only in those large springs close to the sea will extensive invasions of saltwater fishes occur. Only large springs are capable of supporting and feeding their great numbers. Nevertheless, even small springs hundreds of miles from the sea may have saltwater visitors of one type or another, and the great majority of springs have some form of long-term saltwater resident.

In addition to a spring's proximity to the sea, the type of visitor and its length of stay depends upon a species' tolerance to fresh water. Most fishes, whether freshwater or saltwater inhabitants, are strictly confined to their respective medium. The relatively few fishes having the ability to move from one to the other, called "euryhaline" species, are primarily saltwater fishes. An extremely limited number of freshwater fishes can survive in the sea.

Among those saltwater fishes entering the springs, there is varying tolerance to the foreign environment of fresh water. Many oceanic visitors visible in the springs will stay only a short time and then must leave in order to survive. Others will stay for months and then leave to spawn in the sea. A very few remain permanently with the capability of reproducing in fresh water.

Hogchoker Sole
Few fishes of salt water or fresh water have the ability to camouflage themselves as well as the hogchoker. Its presence in almost all of Florida's ocean-access springs goes virtually unnoticed. Except when disturbed by a swimmer's foot or its sudden emergence from the sand to attack prey, it lies motionless and invisible.
(Also called southern sole)
Ichetucknee Springs State Park, Columbia County
Photo by Tim Whitney

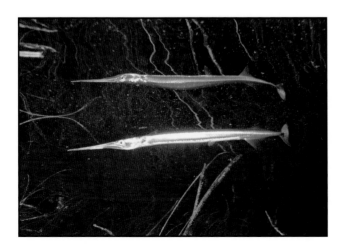

Atlantic Needlefish
Sleek, swordlike and swift as an arrow, a needlefish cruises just under the surface where its doubled image and silver coloration confuse its prey. With its sharp, needlelike beak, it can become a disconcerting darting lance when disoriented by night divers' lights. Similar to the mullet in its complete invasion of Florida's springs, the needlefish, unlike mullet, can reproduce in fresh water, maintaining populations far from the sea.
(Also called saltwater gar, needlegar)
July Spring, Gilchrist County

Gray Snapper
Invading coastal springs and rivers in schools of thousands, gray snappers in great hovering schools hang at entrances to subterranean caves while others seek more confined niches in the dark reaches of caves. This group huddles tightly together in cramped quarters of limestone while a thousand others suspend in open water outside. (Also called black snapper, mangrove snapper) King's Spring, Crystal River National Wildlife Refuge, Citrus County

Blue Crab
Encountered at night, a nocturnal blue crab prepares for battle with reared pincers. Blue crabs, in comparison to other saltwater visitors and residents of springs, have no equal in their tolerance to the extremes of both salt water and fresh water. They can survive in saltwater pools twice as saline as the ocean, and they thrive in freshwater lakes and rivers in such abundance as to be harvested commercially. Their adaptability to fresh water allows large populations to inhabit the St. Johns River system and Lake George as well as springs near Florida's Gulf coast. Crystal River, Citrus County

Crevalle Jack
Surrounded by sheepshead, large and impressive crevalle jacks cruise outside the glass of Homosassa's underwater observatory. Among the swiftest of saltwater gamefish, jacks often invade Homosassa Springs in tremendous numbers, much to the delight of observatory occupants. (Also called jack crevalle, cavally)
Homosassa Springs State Wildlife Park, Citrus County

American Shad
An anadramous species like the salmon, this speeding oceanic shad has journeyed almost 200 miles upstream through several rivers finally to appear in the headspring pool at Silver Springs. Its spawning completed, it will retrace its long course downstream to the Atlantic Ocian.
(Also called blue shad)
Silver Springs, Marion County

Pinfish
Reflecting a late afternoon sun into flashes of silver, pinfish at the vanguard of a large school enter the headspring of a river near the Gulf of Mexico. When pinfish do arrive in spring waters, they appear in immense numbers. Always abundant in oceanic inshore waters, they have notorious abilities at bait stealing and are themselves a common bait used by saltwater anglers.
(Also called pin perch, pig fish, sailor's choice)
King's Spring, Crystal River National Wildlife Refuge, Citrus County

Sheepshead
Shown about to bite a manatee's tail, sheepshead are notorious pests of manatees, picking at propeller wounds or removing parasites from the manatees' skin and inflicting painful bites in the process. Large numbers of sheepshead feeding on a manatee can drive it into dense vegetation to escape its tormentors. Sheepshead, like manatees, are most common in coastal springs during winter when their oceanic waters are much colder than the springs.
(Also called convict fish)
King's Spring, Crystal River National Wildlife Refuge, Citrus County

Striped Bass
A school of striped bass, one of Florida's larger gamefishes in fresh and salt water, cruises the bowl of a headspring pool. Normally an anadromous species entering fresh water to spawn, Florida's inland populations have primarily become permanent river and spring dwellers in the St. Johns River system where they are stocked to maintain populations. So attuned to current, schools have been observed holding position, unable to go further, nose to the bottom, where small spring vents gush from the ground.
(Also called striper, rockfish, linesides)
Silver Glen Springs, Ocala National Forest

Mullet
Undoubtedly the most well-known and abundant saltwater visitors to Florida's fresh waters, mullet are present in or frequently pass through virtually every body of fresh water that has access to the sea. Mullet are the fish often seen jumping several feet in the air, usually three or four times in succession, as they move up rivers and springs. This school, leaving the Suwannee River, moves through a ray of sunlight as it enters a spring run.
(Also called striped mullet, back mullet, jumper, fatback)
Manatee Springs State Park, Levy County
Photo by Tim Whitney

CHAPTER 5

THE FLORIDA MANATEE

"...the bason and stream continually peopled with prodigious numbers and variety of fish and other animals; as the alligator and the manatee or sea cow, in the winter season; part of a skeleton of one, which the Indians had killed last winter, lay upon the banks of the springs; the grinding teeth were about an inch in diameter; the ribs eighteen inches in length, and two inches and a half in thickness, bending with a gentle curve, this bone is esteemed equal to ivory; the flesh of this creature is counted wholesome and pleasant food; the Indians call them by a name which signifies the big beaver. . . ."

William Bartram, 1775

Girl and manatee meet in the headsprings of the Crystal River, the one spring in Florida where divers and manatees can meet in the water. Most agree no better advocates are made for these endangered creatures than swimmers and divers freely approached by these wild ambassadors of their species.
King's Spring, Crystal River National Wildlife Refuge, Citrus County

Manatees are perhaps the inhabitant most unique to the springs of Florida. As most spring inhabitants are immigrants from lakes, rivers and in some cases the ocean into which the springs ultimately flow, manatees have for centuries purposely migrated from cooling winter waters of the Atlantic and Gulf of Mexico to springs and spring-fed rivers that flow into the sea along Florida's coast. In late October or November they enter spring-fed rivers and swim upstream to the river source, seeking refuge in and around the warmer head-springs. Here they remain throughout winter, rarely venturing far if at all into the cold and potentially lethal waters of the ocean.

Manatees occur in Florida at the very northern fringe of their winter range; that they occur here at all is in large part due to the presence of Florida's springs. Cold weather that suddenly drops winter water temperatures below 20°C (68°F) can kill manatees and accounts for the largest number of all natural deaths each year. A major adaptation of manatees that has allowed for their survival in this region has been their historical migrations to warm-water refuges provided by the springs of Florida.

Florida's manatee and the West Indian manatee that ranges the Caribbean and Central and South American coasts to Brazil were long considered a single species. Recent research has determined that Florida's manatee has maintained a distinct population over sufficient time to become a subspecies onto itself, now officially designated the "Florida manatee," *Trichechus manatus latirostris*. The difference between the Florida and West Indian manatees (now designated the "Antillean manatee," *Trichechus manatus manatus*) are slight variations in skull anatomy that are not visually apparent. The springs of Florida have provided a niche critical to maintaining a northern manatee population and have played a role in the continuing process of their evolution.

The Florida manatee is a herbivorous marine mammal and one of only four surviving species of the order Sirenia. The Sirenians were once land mammals that may have been waders feeding upon grasses and aquatic vegetation. After millions of years they returned to the oceans. Their hind legs evolved into a singular large paddle, and their front legs became flippers. But after millenia, evidence of their ancient origins on land prevails. They remain close relatives to the elephant.

In addition to the Antillean manatee, the Amazonian manatee is the only other manatee occurring in the Western Hemisphere and is found only in the fresh waters of the Amazon river and its tributaries. A West African manatee is limited to the coastal waters of West Africa and its major river systems. The remaining Sirenian, the dugong, is an Indo-Pacific species and, unlike the other Sirenians, has a bilobate or two-lobed tail and upper incisors that become tusks in the male. The Bering Straits once held the largest Sirenian, Steller's sea cow. Used for food by Russian fur hunters, this small, isolated and vulnerable population became extinct 27 years after it was discovered by Russian explorers in 1741.

The Florida manatee is the largest spring inhabitant. Adults may reach lengths of 13 feet and weights of more the 3,000 pounds. Along with the other Sirenians, the Florida manatee has one of the heaviest bone structures known, with the longer bones having the characteristics of ivory. The internal placement of heavy bone and lungs gives the manatee perfect aquatic stability along with ballast and list that make it virtually weightless in water. Propelled by moving its broad and flat tail in an up-and-down motion, it moves swiftly with effortless agility and grace. The tail also serves as a rudder and, by adjusting its angle, the manatee can steer, bank and roll its large bulk with relative ease. When the manatee is comparatively motionless as it rests or feeds, the tail angle can also be adjusted to counteract roll and, to some degree, yaw.

The front flippers, designed for precise maneuvering, are kept at the manatee's side as it swims. The manatee is unable to turn its head to the left or right, and the flippers are used primarily to turn its body in the direction it wishes to see or to accurately guide it as it feeds or plays. Near the bottom, its flippers are occasionally used to "walk" and pull its bulk along or push itself from the bottom where the tail then provides speed. The combined use of flippers and tail gives the manatee the ability to perform such hydrobatics as somersaults, half-gainers, head and tail stands, barrel rolls, and upside-down gliding.

Sirenians are air breathers and, with nostrils located on the top end of its elongated face, a manatee merely has to break the water surface with the tip of its snout, take a breath or two, and submerge — a process that can escape notice in all but the calmest of water. These surface intervals usually last less than 5 seconds, while a manatee stays submerged usually 5 to 8 minutes. Though the manatee is capable of staying underwater for as long

A manatee cow and calf, the most famous of Florida's animals, enter a winter sanctuary in the headspring area of the Crystal River. A natural warm-water refuge for thousands of years, Crystal River marks the present-day northernmost limit of the manatee's winter range on the Gulf coast. In some winters it attracts nearly 300 manatees. King's Spring, Crystal River National Wildlife Refuge, Citrus County

as 20 minutes, it is not a deep diver and generally remains near shore or in shallow water even as it roams the oceans.

The manatee is normally a silent animal but communication does occur, most often between a mother and her calf. Their language of high-pitched squeaks, chirps and screams, audible to divers in the water, is usually limited to sudden stress situations or social interaction, and increases when turbid water limits visual contact.

Florida's manatees appear to live lives of relative leisure. While in the springs, they pass away the winter feeding, "playing" or resting. They have no seasonal breeding patterns and mate whenever a female becomes receptive, either at maturity or when she no longer has a dependent calf. The

sexual courtship of the male is a relentless affair of embracing and mouthing that will often drive an unreceptive cow into hiding or force her to run aground in shallow water. More gentle courtship entails kissing. At a female's proper time she mates with more than one male, the most persistent male being the most likely to cause conception. Gestation is thought to be about 400 days.

A manatee cow normally bears only one calf approximately every three years and suckles it with milk glands located under the front flippers. The calf will begin grazing on plants as it enters its second year, but will not reach sexual maturity until it is four to six years old. The life span of manatees is estimated to be around 60. They may live much longer.

Potential natural enemies of the manatee include crocodiles, alligators and sharks. Calves are most vulnerable, but predation appears not to be a significant problem for calves or adults. Adults are large enough to discourage most attacks, and calves are born in sheltered waters or springs and are well protected by their mothers.

With the approach of spring, manatees leave their winter sanctuaries and move into the warming sea. Once in the sea they disperse but remain near the coast, roaming as far north as Virginia and to the west as far as Louisiana. Their presence in ocean shallows, along with their undulating swimming motions and frequent visits to the surface, are thought to have given rise to the legends of mermaids being sighted by tired and lonely sailors.

Manatees congregate in approximately 25 different winter sanctuaries throughout Florida, including many warm-water discharge areas of power plants, but three locations in particular provide ideal areas for observing them in the clear waters of springs. Blue Springs State Park in Volusia County is a winter sanctuary for the St. Johns River population of manatees where they can be observed from docks and shore. In another state park at Homosassa Springs, now a rehabilitation center for sick and injured manatees, wild and contained manatees can be seen in the headspring pool from an underwater observatory. An even greater number of manatees winter in and around the headsprings of the Crystal River, a 45-acre National Wildlife Refuge created to protect and observe a

THE SPRINGS OF FLORIDA

growing winter population. There, manatees can easily be seen from a drifting boat as they swim underneath or feed on vegetation in the clear water. They have no inherent fear of people and, with a calm and gradual apprach, are easily befriended by a diver, often allowing themselves to be scratched or rubbed. Manatees more experienced with divers will frequently roll over at a diver's approach or seek one out, in effect asking that its stomach be rubbed. Calves are especially curious and playful and often approach and follow divers as long as their mothers remain in the area.

A manatee's ability to eat over 100 pounds of aquatic vegetation per day has induced attempts to use them for controlling aquatic plants that clog many lakes, canals and waterways in Florida. The experiments proved to have limited success. The floating water hyacinth, an exotic species accidentally introduced into Florida and one of the major plants it was hoped manatees could control, is not a preferred food if other vegetation is available, as it often is. Manatees also required water deeper than many of the canals and waterways could provide. That, combined with the inability of manatees to withstand cold water, demanded their transport to suitable areas or more southern waters for the winter. Many manatees were injured or died in the process, and the problems outweighted the benefits. Concern by state agencies for manatees and their future in Florida brought these weed-control programs to a close.

Manatees are known to have inhabited the waters of Florida since at least the Pleistocene era, but the future of the manatee has always seemingly been tenuous. For thousands of years, they have been hunted for their meat, oil and leather. Their skin was used for Indian shields and made into whips and walking canes. Great hunting parties once sailed from Cuba to Florida waters in search of abundant seafood that included manatees.

As early as the 1700s, Florida was declared a manatee sanctuary by the then ruling English. Early scientists, naturalists and writers of the late 1800s predicted its extinction. By 1907, the state of Florida passed a law prohibiting the continued killing of manatees. Still, during the Depression and early war years, many were killed for food, and even now an occasional manatee is found butchered. Protection of the Florida manatee was extended further by the Marine Mammal Act of 1972, the Endangered Species Act of 1973 and the Florida Manatee Sanctuary Act of 1978 that makes the entire state a manatee sanctuary and designates the manatee as the state marine mammal. Today, with a population that fluctuates around 1500, the Florida manatee is not in imminent danger of extinction, but it remains an endangered species with an uncertain future.

The greatest number of human-related manatee deaths in present-day Florida are the result of collisions with watercraft. Manatees that survive the collisions often bear the telltale parallel scars inflicted by propellors. While most deaths occur when they congregate in their confining winter sanctuaries, if given an opportunity, they can readily avoid such collisions. The hazards of such a collision are not solely limited to the manatee. Many boaters can attest to damages incurred in the impact of hitting a 2,000-pound manatee.

Among many efforts to reduce the number of manatee fatalities due to watercraft, federal and state natural resource agencies are posting boat speed restrictions and warning signs noting the presence of manatees. Other organizations, corporate and private, are sponsoring informational programs that educate the public who share Florida waters with manatees with the message that man and manatee can exist together.

Another significant factor affecting today's population of the Florida manatee is that its preferred waters for food and habitat are also preferred for development by Florida's fast-growing human population. This gradual loss of its natural range in addition to accidental deaths will affect most the presence of manatees in the springs of Florida through the 21st century.

From the air, several manatees wintering in the Homosassa River can be seen bunched up at a temporary fence that prevents their entry into the deep headspring pool just feet away. For the manatees' safety, the fence was installed during repair of an underwater observatory visible to the left in the headspring. A white rectangular holding pen used in manatee research and rehabilitation is visible next to the observatory.
Homosassa Springs State Wildlife Park, Citrus County

THE FLORIDA MANATEE

CHAPTER 6

Spring Parks

"This amazing and delightful scene, though real, appears at first but as a piece of excellent painting; there seems no medium; you imagine the picture to be within a few inches of your eyes, and that you may without the least difficulty touch any one of the fish, or put your finger upon the crocodile's eye, when it is really twenty or thirty feet underwater. . . ."

William Bartram, 1775

One of Weeki Wachee's famed mermaids offers a snack of bread to native members of the cast, tamed by the daily presence of "people" in their midst. The origins of mermaid shows and underwater theatre are in this headspring pool of Weeki Wachee Springs.
Weeki Wachee Springs, Hernando County
Photo by Tim Whitney

Bartram would surely envy an audience that watches mermaids underwater in the blue glow of Weeki Wachee Spring. In fascination they see in a way Bartram never could the color and vibrancy of these places. There is a sense of wonder here that bridges the gap of centuries. Though we understand them now and can explain them, that fascination for these places endures and has evolved into diverse parks and enterprises that, each in a different way, attract us and allow a closer look into some of the world's most alluring fresh waters. For anyone of any age, where face mask, fins and canoes are not always required, there are journeys here over and through this underwater world.

Florida has a wealth of natural resources in the abundant environments found between the panhandle and the Keys. In concerted efforts to preserve parts of Florida's wild heritage, the spring environments have found special favor in that many of them have been permanently set aside as parks and recreation areas across the state. Created and protected by every level of government from federal to municipal, spring parks are as varied in size and form as the springs they protect. Major springs are the centerpieces of four national forest recreation areas. Of Florida's 114 state parks and recreation areas, 12 encompass springs and spring rivers, and other spring sites are under consideration. And many smaller springs that have for 200 years been local fishing and swimming holes will always remain those special places as county and village parks.

At other springs, the advent of private dive resorts, campgrounds and canoe rental outlets with admission fees and guidelines was at first a discouraging sight to a generation of divers, campers and canoers used to spring sites as places wild and free. But as the growing attraction of Florida's springs brought an ever-increasing number of visitors with varied interests, some springs were turning into dumps littered with trash, spring banks were eroding away, and some springs were vandalized, their fish speared and surrounding trees chopped down. In springs where commercial ventures have appeared, the preservation of those springs is essential to making them more spectacular places to visit, more accessible and easier to experience. In the end most will agree that commercial springs are there for all of us to enjoy, and are worth the price.

WEST CENTRAL (map, pages 82-83)

In the center of springs country, a spring with the largest known flow in the world has always been Florida's most famous spring attraction — **Silver Springs**, in business now for more than 100 years. Perhaps Spanish explorers were the first tourists to Silver Springs, where the hull of a small boat thought to be of Spanish origin still lies on the bottom of the spring. The first real trade in tourism began in the mid-1800s when visitors came by stagecoach and pole barge. As its acclaim spread, a steamboat line developed to haul cargo and passengers up the winding Oklawaha and Silver rivers, passing dense forest and abundant alligators to finally arrive at the source of the spring's ever-increasing fame.

The invention of the glass-bottom boat in the late 1800s opened a new window to the springs environment. Underwater views of the spring had until then been limited to holding glass and clear

Made of sturdy cypress, a boat thought to be of Spanish origin has been preserved on the bottom of Silver Springs for perhaps as long as 400 years. Whoever its builders were, it was surely used for a better look into Florida's first tourist attraction.
Silver Springs, Marion County
Photo by Tim Whitney

bottles through the water's surface. When a young John Morrell fit a piece of glass in the bottom of a rowboat at Silver Springs, a new industry was born. By 1903, his business grew so large a suit was instituted against him to prevent his many passengers from crowding the railroad wharves at the spring.

The environs of Silver Springs have changed in the last century, but because of its park status, the spring itself has changed little. Underwater, inside the enormous cave below the glass-bottom boat docks, the fossil bones of Pleistocene beasts litter the floor, undisturbed for 10,000 years. Now a national landmark, Silver Springs is a 350-acre multi-theme park where glass-bottom boats are still the main attraction. Visitors to Silver Springs today will also find boat tours of the Silver River and land and water tours through free-roaming wildlife. A petting zoo is provided to introduce children to wildlife, and live animal presentations educate and entertain.

More people have seen Silver Springs than they may realize. It has been portrayed as jungle, forest and ocean in more than 30 motion pictures, including James Bond and Tarzan films, "The Creature from the Black Lagoon," and in over 100 episodes of Lloyd Bridges' "Sea Hunt."

The river formed by Silver Springs has recently become the **Silver River State Park**, one of the Florida Park system's newer acquisitions. The park protects four miles of rare waterway lined with wildlife and forest. Not yet open to the public, the park will offer travelers a journey over and in one of the world's most transparent rivers.

Another recent spring park created by the Florida Park Service, **Rainbow Springs State Park**, has encompassed the headwaters of the Rainbow River, another of Florida's larger spring rivers. The headspring area, hundreds of feet wide and 15 feet deep, pushes water through countless small vents and bubbling sands to create one of Florida's largest

Silver Springs Cave
Framed by the entrance to its algae-rimmed cave, Silver Springs floats a glass-bottom boat 60 feet above on invisible waters. The cave funnels more than a half billion gallons of water each day into the spring, making Silver Springs the largest in the world in terms of average flow.
Silver Springs, Marion County

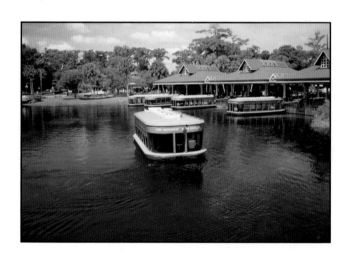

Glass-Bottom Boat
A glass-bottom boat floats over the headspring pool in Silver Springs, in identical position as the boat pictured underwater. With these electric-powered craft named after Seminole chiefs, Silver Springs sails the world's largest fleet of glass-bottomed boats.
Silver Springs, Marion County

Homosassa Observatory
To everyone's delight, the close pass of a wild manatee is an exciting moment for visitors to Homosassa Spring's underwater observatory. Manatees and great numbers of large oceanic fishes moving back and forth from Gulf to spring are visible daily from this observatory unique in Florida's springs.
Homosassa Springs State Wildlife Park, Citrus County

In one of the world's most unusual diving parks, visitors to the underground cavern at Devils Den want to know more about this unique place from the diver just completing his underwater look at the cave. The hole above easily explains why scientists have recovered a great number of fossilized bones from this site, for thousands of years a trap for any creature falling in.
Devils Den, Levy County

spring pools abundant with spring life and displaying a variety of aquatic plants. Once a snorkeler's paradise, it offered underwater vistas of distance unequaled in the springs of Florida, where underwater visibility exceeding 200 feet is common. Now open only on weekends, the spring is closed to snorkeling as park policies are being studied. Snorkelers hope the public will be allowed to see that the most rare and unique beauty of Rainbow Springs is found not in the land around the spring but beneath its surface.

Just a mile downstream from the park, the state has also recently purchased what was long known as the Rainbow River Campground. Now officially titled the **Rainbow River State Campground**, the park offers complete camping, RV facilities and canoe rentals at the river's edge. Across the river, the **KP Hole County Park** also provides canoes and a roped-in swimming area. This area of the river is known by divers for the many fossil bones and teeth of Pleistocene mastodons, horses, and sloths found in the bottom sands.

The Florida park system's aggressive, sometimes controversial land and springs acquisition policies have resulted in the creation of new state parks around some of Florida's most rare and extraordinary springs, and in the process have blurred the old definitions and traditional concepts of what makes a state park. One of these is Homosassa Springs; what was once a large tourist attraction now has become **Homosassa Springs State Wildlife Park**, one of the most unusual and educational state parks in the country.

The headspring pool at Homosassa Springs has always been and still remains the center attraction. There, floating in 55 feet of water and weighing 168 tons, rests an underwater observatory unlike any other in fresh water. Through large plate glass windows that line the structure, the spring's many inhabitants, including manatees, swim the deep pool and circle the observatory in full view of a captivated audience.

Florida's manatees have historically been attracted to Homosassa in winter for its 74^0 F waters. Now, as a research and rehabilitation center for injured and sick manatees, Homosassa Springs is the only place in Florida where the general public can view wild manatees year-round from an underwater perspective, something before reserved to the domain of snorkelers and divers.

Because of the spring's close proximity to the sea, saltwater fishes visit the headspring in great numbers and variety, partially due to the spring water's relatively high salt content. Crevalle jack, sheepshead and sea catfish that continuously circle the observatory are usually the most abundant. Snook, large tarpon and manatees occasionally make impressive passes only inches from the observatory.

As a showcase for native Florida wildlife and endangered species, the park presents live animal encounters and informative programs with manatees, crocodiles, alligators, snakes and birds. A day at Homosassa Springs can be an exceptional spring and wildlife experience.

Thirty miles north there is **Devils Den**, one of the world's most unusual swimming and dive sites. Unlike no other commercial site in Florida, the waters of Devils Den are underground at the bottom of a large, dry cave, accessible through a stairway cut into surrounding rock, then down wooden steps to a crystal pool 120 feet wide.

A small section of the cave ceiling collapsed thousands of years ago, exposing a hole in the level ground above. For centuries afterward, Devils Den was a trap with no escape, evidenced by fossil bones found here of Pleistocene bears, giant sloths and great wolves. Human bones at this site indicate they too fell victim to its trap or used the cave as a burial site more than 8,000 years ago. On cold winter mornings, steam rising through the ceiling hole from warm water below gave early settlers reason for naming this site more than a hundred years ago. Today it's a place to safely enjoy a unique kind of swimming and diving along with picnic areas and horseback riding around the extensive grounds.

Blue Grotto, just a few miles from Devils Den, is a well-known inland dive and training site. Below its sizeable open water area is the largest accessible clearwater cavern dive in Florida, where certified divers are allowed to enter up to the limits of a permanently installed safety line. Blue Grotto is a safe and exciting dive in a natural sink-syphon with depths to 110 feet. Surface light is always present in its cobalt-blue water, but guides are available to escort divers if requested. Along with an on-site dive shop, RV and tent camping is available.

Further east and just south of Ocala, **Paradise Spring** offers an unusual opportunity for divers to view the fossil-rich walls of what is actually a crystal-clear sinkhole. From an opening just 20 feet across at the surface, the pool opens up underwater into cavern rooms that extend to 140-foot depths. Sand dollars, sea biscuits, and the ribs and bones of a

Upon their emergence from a spring, divers answering the questions of curious onlookers is a common occurrence in Florida. Here at Blue Grotto, divers tell of one of Florida's largest and clearest cavern dives extending 110 feet below where they stand.
Blue Grotto, Levy County

giant sea creature protrude from the walls, preserved since they died there on a shallow reef 60 million years ago.

One of Florida's deeper sinks is available to divers for specialty training at Hal Watt's **Forty Fathom Grotto** near Ocala. Open by appointment, the sink is used primarily as a training facility for deep dive and advanced diving techniques to depths of 240 feet, using both compressed air and mixed breathing gases. Escorted dive tours at safe depths are available to any certified diver. Hal Watt holds the world-record deep dive in fresh water using compressed air, a feat achieved in another Florida sink at a depth of 415 feet. Watt's philosophy of using compressed air beyond the recommended safe depth of 130 feet has met with controversy from other diver certifying organizations.

SOUTH CENTRAL (map, pages 82-83)

The most southern region of Florida where springs are found produces springs of extreme contrast, and two springs are world-famous because of it. One is **Warm Mineral Springs**, the southernmost and rarest form of spring in Florida.

Warm Mineral Springs is a Florida spring attraction known around the world but for reasons very different from the others. Unlike any other spring in the state, Warm Mineral Springs is Florida's only truly warm spring open to the public, issuing nine million gallons of water per day at a constant 87°F. Its southernmost location of all springs, its warm temperature and high mineral content reveal a source for this spring far deeper in the aquifer than any northern spring. Interestingly, despite the water's warmth and high salt and sulphur content, mosquitofish inhabit the surface of this spring in unusual profusion.

Warm Mineral Springs also has unique archaeological significance. Evidence of human presence has been found here underwater along its slope that extends to depths of 250 feet. Carbon-dated skeletal remains preserved in the mineral-rich water reveal that prehistoric peoples lived at this spring more than 10,000 years ago, coexisting with sabre cats and giant sloths.

That warm, mineral-rich water has attracted visitors for centuries. They now come from the world over to bathe in spring water many claim has properties to heal and restore vigor. Listed in the National Register of Historic Places, Warm Mineral Springs has become a resort and health spa where more than half its visitors arrive from other countries. Seeking spring legends and cures for muscular problems, arthritis and rheumatism, many bathers profess finding relief in this water that has five times the mineral content of all other famous spas around the world. Its property as a certain and immediate laxative if its sulphur-rich waters are swallowed is unquestioned.

A nearby spring, **Little Salt Spring**, is the one other warm water spring in the state. Found to hold a rare abundance of fossils and human artifacts, more than any other spring in Florida, its 200-foot depths are intensively studied and closed to the public.

Included among many spectacular discoveries in the spring was the shell of an extinct giant land tortoise, 12 feet in diameter, found with a wooden stake driven through it. The tortoise had evidently been killed with the stake, overturned and cooked in its shell. Carbon dating revealed the tortoise may have been several centuries old before being killed by a Paleo-Indian 12,000 years ago. The shell and spear represent the earliest known evidence of humans in Florida.

The other well-known spring in this region is **Weeki Wachee Springs**, a large first-magnitude spring that attracts visitors from around the world for a unique look into its underwater domain.

In 1946, Newton Perry, an ex-Navy frogman with an idea and an affinity for another kind of water legend, purchased the land around the spring and built an underwater theatre 15 feet below the surface — the first of its kind. The following year he presented his vision to the public, the first live underwater mermaid show. And for almost 50 years since, the show goes on.

Weeki Wachee, "City of Mermaids," has been the home of more than 400 mermaids in its long history of providing underwater theatre and ballet. Mermaids — and now mermen — surrounded by a native cast, perform their routines behind three layers of safety glass separating them from their audience. The theatre now seats 400 people 16 feet underwater with a panoramic view of the Weeki Wachee River headspring source.

Through the years, Weeki Wachee has grown into a 200-acre family entertainment theme park. Informative river cruises are provided to its Pelican Preserve, a refuge for injured birds, and educational programs with live exotic birds and birds of prey are presented. A wildlife petting zoo gives children an opportunity to experience deer, emus and other wildlife close up. Buccaneer Bay, next to Weeki Wachee, is a newly developed six-acre water park, the only natural spring water park in Florida.

Recently acquired as a National Forest Recreation Area, Silver Glen Springs is a swimmer's and snorkeler's delight. A half-mile from Lake George, schools of striped bass and African tilapia can be seen here in an abundance rarely found elsewhere. Silver Glen Springs, Ocala National Forest

Visitors to Warm Mineral Springs can swim in very warm, mineral-rich water, unique among the springs of Florida. Visitors journey here from around the world to drink and bathe in its waters in search of relief from a variety of ailments. From a source far deeper than others in the state, the spring's flow of nine million gallons per day creates a 2¹/₂-acre lake more than 250 feet deep.
Warm Mineral Springs, Sarasota County

CENTRAL (map, page 81)

The central area of Florida just north of Orlando is a region rich in forests, lakes and large spring parks. Here, within the Ocala National Forest, the oldest national forest east of the Mississippi River, four major national forest spring recreation areas and 36,000 acres of spring-fed lakes can be found. Two of these springs, Alexander and Silver Glen, are first-magnitude springs, forming clear spring streams that flow to the St. Johns River and Lake George, respectively.

Alexander Springs has the greatest flow of any natural spring on U.S. Government land, forming a large deep pool ideal for swimmers, snorkelers and divers. Surrounded by extensive wilderness, Alexander Springs can reveal an abundance of

wildlife above and below the water not often found in other public-access springs. The seven-mile Alexander Creek formed by the spring is a popular wilderness canoe trail, and canoes and camping sites are available at the spring. An inviting nature trail circles around the spring and through subtropical forest.

The **Silver Glen National Forest Recreation Area** around first-magnitude Silver Glen Springs is a new addition to the national forest. Once a large, private campground, the spring is now being managed to return it to a wilderness environment, and swimming and snorkeling are the only activities available. But with its short run to Lake George, Silver Glen can be a spectacular spring for snorkelers when huge schools of striped bass move

Once advertised as the "fountain of youth" with waters "impregnated with a deliciously healthy combination of soda and sulphur," DeLeon Springs has always been an active place. Here, a rafted swimmer has been watching from above while a group of divers take a training course below. DeLeon Springs State Recreation Area, Volusia County

The Juniper Springs Canoe Trail flows through seven miles of semitropical forest found in no other national forest in the continental United States. To protect people, vegetation and wildlife, travelers are restricted to using canoes or kayaks and no wading is allowed. Juniper Springs, Ocala National Forest

from the lake into the headspring pool or when great numbers of large African tilapia invade the headspring area to build nests and spawn.

Within the **Salt Springs National Forest Recreation Area**, the headspring pool offers another phenomenon to snorkelers. A combination of freshwater and saltwater vents flowing into the headspring area creates a "halocline," causing unusual visual distortions of objects viewed underwater. Campgrounds and extensive hiking trails are available around the spring, and the long Salt Springs Run that flows to Lake George is one of the better fishing and boating areas in the forest.

Juniper Springs is one of the oldest and best known national forest recreation areas in the eastern United States. Built in the 1930s by the Civilian Conservation Corps, its headspring pool has always been a popular place to swim and snorkel, and its camping areas accommodate everything from tents to motor homes. But it is the seven-mile canoe trail

formed by Juniper Springs and nearby **Fern Hammock Springs** that has unique significance to travelers by kayak or canoe. One of the clearest canoe trails in Florida, the spring stream flows through a wilderness semitropical forest not found in any other national forest in the continental United States. It is a wild and scenic trip through dense vegetation; for reasons of safety, only kayaks and canoes are permitted on the spring run. To protect people, snakes and alligators from each other, no floats, tubes or rafts are allowed.

Florida's state park system offers a great array of spring types and activities among the many forms of springs it manages. The four state parks in this region vary greatly and some are rich in history with legends of sacred waters and fountains of youth and stories of battles waged in the settlement of Florida.

The spring that forms the **DeLeon Springs State Recreation Area** was "sacred water" to its ancient visitors. Early Spanish explorers, possibly

There are many forms of smaller, less-well-known campgrounds, fishing camps and RV resorts tucked away among smaller springs and spring-fed rivers and lakes. Here, Blue Springs Campground is busy on a hot summer's day.
Blue Springs, Gilchrist County

Ponce de León himself, occupied the area in the early 1500s.

Three hundred years later the Seminole Indians briefly gained control of the spring from early settlers during the Second Seminole War. The spring was the center of battle again during the Civil War when Union troops captured the spring and destroyed its sugarmill. As the spring became better known in the 1880s, advertisements aimed at northern tourists promised a fountain of youth "impregnated with a deliciously healthy combination of soda and sulphur." Today the spring is dammed to form a popular swimming and picnic park.

Another spring dammed to form a popular swimming area forms the heart of the **Wekiwa**

Springs State Park. The spring is the source of the Wekiwa River, a clear water canoe trail through 15 miles of remote Florida before joining the St. Johns River. Miles of horse trails that wind through the park provide a glimpse of Florida as Bartram would have seen it.

The **Rock Springs Run State Reserve** is thousands of acres of state land next to Wekiwa Springs that has been set aside as a primitive area. Rock Springs Run joins the Wekiwa River in this remote reserve where travelers journey only by foot, canoe or horseback.

The source of Rock Springs Run has long been preserved in **Kelly Park**, managed by the Orange County Parks and Recreation Department. The spring flows from a rock cliff to create one of the

The blue hue of Madison Blue's headspring pool behind them, two fully equipped cave divers begin their journey into one of the world's most extensive underwater cave systems. Visitors to this realm are trained to always position themselves near cave ceilings where their depth is as shallow as possible, a technique that conserves their air and avoids disturbing silt from the cave floor.

Madison Blue Springs Resort, Madison County

most scenic and pleasant swimming areas in the state of Florida.

One of Florida's more enjoyable springs for divers and snorkelers can be found in **Blue Springs State Park**. The spring rises from a vertical shaft and gives divers and snorkelers alike an understanding of the forces and volume of first-magnitude flow. A short, clear run flows to the St. Johns River. Blue Springs is also an official manatee sanctuary where the St. Johns River population of manatees congregate in winter. They can be observed here but not encountered by swimming or boat.

NORTH CENTRAL (map, page 84)

Most of the many springs of northern Florida rise to the surface at the very edge of or near the region's three major rivers — the Suwannee and its two large tributaries, the Withlacoochee and Santa Fe. In the process of eroding away surface layers of clay, the rivers have exposed breaches in the limestone bedrock from which springs can appear. In the process of these same rivers flooding, they may have helped create perhaps the largest system of interconnected underwater caves in the world.

The first-magnitude spring at **Madison Blue Springs Resort** is a good example. There, the spring rises at the edge of the Withlacoochee River when the river is at its normal level. When the river floods, it inundates the spring by several feet and reverses the spring's flow, in the process pouring great volumes of slightly acidic river water deep into the aquifer. Over the course of many thousands of years this continuous cycle has dissolved deep pathways into the limestone source of Madison Blue and other springs in the area. As a result, cave explorers in Madison Blue have so far discovered more than 35,000 feet of passageways, making it one of the most extensive underwater cave systems known. Its tunnels continue on unexplored into the aquifer.

Madison Blue has recently been developed, with diving and other park facilities available on site. With camping, canoe rentals, airfills, bathhouses and cottages planned, Madison Blue can accommodate everyone from swimmers and novice snorkelers to the most advanced cave diver.

Many years of neglect had left the spring with its banks eroding away, allowing the Withlacoochee River to more easily flood it with each passing year. Since the spring's new ownership, many improvements have already been made and others are planned to restore the spring to its natural state. With its remote location on one of Florida's most scenic rivers, a brilliant blue and rare spring rises among live oak and cypress, preserved now for everyone who loves wild Florida.

Further downstream, along the Suwannee River, another major spring system can be found at **Peacock Springs**, one of Florida's more beautiful spring sites where its blue pool is almost hidden within ancient floodplain forest.

The recent acquisition of Peacock Springs as a state recreation area is of special significance to divers. Notorious for the "commando dives" that would occur even when the spring was closed when on private property, and known well too for its legacy as a killer spring for the 47 divers lost in its maze, Peacock is now protected at last. Its two-spring, six-sink complex is one of the most extensive underwater cave systems known and among the longest in the United States. More than 28,000 feet of its passageways have been explored and mapped. With diving in Peacock's cave now monitored and restricted to certified cave divers, its dark legacy to divers has ended at last.

Much further down the river near where the Suwannee meets the Gulf of Mexico, the first-magnitude spring at **Manatee Springs State Park** still offers refuge to an occasional manatee, but more often its cool deep headspring attracts swimmers, divers and snorkelers. William Bartram visited

Canoers take a welcome detour from a Suwannee River journey and paddle up a short spring run to its source in Manatee Springs State Park. A large, first-magnitude spring, it derives its name from the occasional visits by manatees described by Bartram here during his travels two centuries ago.
Manatee Springs State Park, Levy County

The Ichetucknee River, known for its beautiful springs and streams, is famous for the two-knot current that carries tubers through miles of wild Florida. So popular has this journey become, a shuttle service is now provided as part of the park entrance fee.
Ichetucknee Springs State Park

The large open area of Vortex Spring has become a multiactivity park. While swimmers, canoers and sunbathers occupy the far shallow end of the spring, divers underwater are undergoing training while others swim in the cavern with shadow bass and eels.
Vortex Spring, Holmes County

THE SPRINGS OF FLORIDA

and named the spring 200 years ago, and the spring is still a welcome place to rest and camp for canoers on passage down the Suwannee River.

In the eastern part of this region, another state park is known for the journey it provides. **Ichetucknee Springs State Park** is known the world over for the number of visitors who float the spring river on innertubes for miles through woodland preserve. The park offers a shuttle service to accommodate its many visitors, sometimes numbering thousands per day on a hot summer weekend.

Nine named springs add to the stream's flow in its course through the park where many kinds of fish, turtles and birds can be observed in and around the water. Once famous to divers for the many fossils found by floating the stream, fossil collecting is no longer permitted in any state park.

Two springs along the Suwannee are county parks that offer picnic and recreation areas along the spring and river. **Mayo Blue Spring Park** in Lafayette County does not allow scuba diving in the spring where a dangerous underwater cave system extends more than 20,000 feet away from the entrance. **Hart Spring County Park** in Gilchrist County is also a family recreation park where a large spring and run to the Suwannee River provide enjoyable swimming and snorkeling. Not far away in the town of Branford, a quiet municipal park around **Branford Springs** at the river's edge has been used for picnics and swimming for hundreds of years.

Two private spring parks along the Suwannee River attract a variety of travelers. Canoers, campers and divers all meet at **River Rendezvous** with Convict Spring at its center. This large wooded site is complete with lodging, campground, restaurant and a dive shop offering shuttle bus runs to the nearby Peacock Springs system as well as boat charters to local springs, some of which are only accessible by river.

A large, full-facility RV resort and campground at Otter Springs hosts thousands of visitors each year with its scenic spring and lowland forest along the river. In 1992, **Otter Springs** was the site of an unprecedented event in the history of scuba diving in the springs of Florida. Four divers, untrained and unequipped for cave diving, entered Otter's headspring cave. Within a short distance they stirred up the cave's silt and were immediately lost and disoriented in an enveloping black cloud. By pure chance one of the divers, in a panic, swam blindly into the entrance and surfaced for help. Also by chance, one of Florida's foremost cave divers and

explorers, Woody Jasper, was attending a company picnic at Otter Springs that day. His diving gear in his truck, Jasper quickly entered the cave to find one diver already dead on the cave floor. The two others were nearly unconscious, breathing from a small pocket of foul air trapped at the cave ceiling. Sharing his air, Jasper returned them to the surface one at a time, the only time divers lost in a Florida cave were rescued instead of their bodies being recovered.

A great number of springs also rise in and around the Santa Fe River along its winding course to the Suwannee. Gilchrist County recently acquired **Poe Springs** and changed it from an eroding spring suffering from misuse and neglect to a pleasant family park. Nearby **Blue Springs Campground** has long been a local favorite for a summer swim and a quiet place to camp during Florida's winter.

Among the very first diving parks to appear in Florida was **Ginnie Springs**, now one of America's best diving and camping resorts. Situated among a nine-springs group along the Santa Fe, Ginnie Springs has some of the best spring diving, snorkeling and immense cavern and cave dives found anywhere and attracts visitors from around the world. With a large dive shop, equipment rentals ranging from canoes to dive masks, and camping from RVs to wilderness sites, Ginnie Springs offers a great variety of opportunities to enjoy the many kinds of springs and river wilderness found in this region of Florida.

PANHANDLE (map, page 85)

The panhandle region of Florida does not have a great abundance of springs, but what spring parks it has are among the finest. One of the first diving parks to appear in Florida was at **Vortex Spring** near the small town of Ponce de Leon. Vortex's large spring basin and cave have made it popular for diver training with its underwater platforms and airbell suspended below the surface. With a full range of camping facilities, lodges and rental equipment available, Vortex accommodates thousands of visitors each year, many of whom come just to swim in its clear water. Divers can always find the rare shadowbass within the first cavern room in the blue dim of ambient light.

Not far from Vortex is **Morrison Springs**, long known by divers for its huge cavern populated by hundreds of eels. And not far from Morrison is fossil-rich **Cypress Springs**, a small, beautiful spring rising among lowland cypress. Its pristine

A first-time snorkeler reaches out to her first creature sighted underwater in Ginnie Springs. The many springs, depths, caves and caverns along with easy entries to the water make Ginnie Springs an attractive learning environment for novices at all levels of springs exploration.

Ginnie Springs Resort, Gilchrist County

cavern descends to depths of 70 feet, and the spring basin is among Florida's most scenic. The spring also provides camping and canoe rentals and pickup for float trips down the spring run and Holmes Creek.

Another private spring park is just east of Marianna where **Blue Springs** offers a family recreation park around the headspring pool. The flow from Blue Springs has been dammed five miles downstream to form a clear and narrow lake called Merrits Mill Pond. The largest redear sunfish in Florida are found here.

The three remaining spring parks in the panhandle are part of the state of Florida parks system: **Ponce de Leon State Recreation Area** is a small, quiet preserve of nature trails where the spring area is used for picnics and swimming. The **Florida Caverns State Park** was not created

because of a spring, but a large and beautiful spring named Blue Hole flows from the park to the Chipola River. The park does give revealing tours through its surface caverns created in similar form and fashion to the many more underwater caverns beneath your feet.

The designation to state park status of Wakulla Springs, the deepest and largest spring in the world, is another unusual and fortunate spring acquisition by the Florida Park Service. Now officially titled the **Edward Ball Wakulla Springs State Park**, the spring and surrounding 3,000 acres south of Talla-hassee had, since the 1930s, been a private estate and wildlife refuge owned by financier and conser-vationist Edward Ball. As a result of its refuge status and later as a tourist attraction, Wakulla Springs and its grounds have been among the longest and most

A fish-eye's view from 100 feet underwater silhouettes a Wakulla Springs snorkel diver against clouds and sky. As escorted snorkelers float above the deepest headspring in the world, they can view dimensions of depth and an abundance of creatures found in no other spring or park in the world.
Wakulla Springs State Park, Wakulla County

extensively protected spring areas in Florida, an accomplishment reflected in the natural abundance of vegetation and wildlife on land and in the great size and multitudes of underwater inhabitants that roam its waters.

Wakulla Springs has vistas unequaled in the springs of Florida. The spring terrain is visible from the surface to depths of more than 150 feet. Fishes inhabit the spring virtually by the thousands, and turtles and alligators move about undisturbed as they have for centuries. The spring environment unfolds beneath the keels of glass-bottom boats as they cruise the river environment and complete their journey over the main spring. And at the spring's deepest corner, hidden from the surface beneath the overhang of a limestone cliff, a dark entrance leads into Wakulla's immense cave.

The cave system that funnels Wakulla's water to the surface is the largest known underwater cave in the world. Beginning at 180 feet, the cave opening appears at the base of a steep, sandy slope. A singular tunnel descends southeast into limestone and turns sharply to the southwest where all light disappears. An arched ceiling undulates down the tunnel tightening in areas to heights of five feet and rising in other places to spacious heights of 100 feet. The tunnel floor, 70 to 150 feet wide, holds scattered remnants of bones of mastodons and sloths, and charcoal remains of fires indicate the presence of Ice-Age peoples when water levels were lower and the cave was dry. In 1987, an ambitious and remarkable expedition was begun to explore and chart Wakulla's subterranean spring tunnel to the limits of existing technology. Divers riding propulsion vehicles and breathing mixed gases mapped more than 10,000 feet of underwater tunnels, some extending to depths of 320 feet. Wakulla's main tunnel was explored to 3,300 feet from its entrance, and four new major site tunnels were discovered and mapped, one to a horizontal distance of 4,176 feet. Four of the five tunnels continue on beyond the limits of this last exploration. New expeditions being planned will venture further and deeper into the source of this largest spring in the world.

The tremendous size of the subterranean river that flows from the cave accounts for Wakulla Spring's flow rates, the world's largest, exceeding one billion gallons per day at peak periods. The spring's flow fluctuates greatly, however, and is normally less than Silver Spring's record average flow. Heavy rains can affect the spring to a dramatic degree when underground tunnels with access to local surface streams leak into the main tunnel, allowing dark, tannic river waters to pour from the cave entrance.

In addition to glass-bottom boat tours, the park service runs wildlife observation boat tours downstream among ancient cypress trees, remarkable bird life and some of the largest wild alligators in Florida. Swimming is a popular activity in the park but, for safety reasons, is permitted only in a limited area of the headspring. Venturing outside the designated swimming area is prohibited, and access to the river anywhere within the park is restricted to official tour boats only.

A 27-room Spanish-style lodge built in 1937 by Edward Ball provides an unusual and pleasant opportunity for visitors to stay on the park grounds.

The lodge features ornate ceilings, marble floors and antique furniture of the age. An old-fashioned soda fountain is open for business in the lodge, which also includes a fine dining room. The lodge and dining facilities serve also as an attractive conference center operated by the Florida State University Center for Professional Development and Public Service.

The philosophy and objective of the Florida Park Service has been to preserve the "original natural Florida," and state parks are managed to the extent possible to appear as they did when the first Europeans arrived. In few other spring parks is original natural Florida more available for the experience than in Wakulla Springs.

The often-asked-about underwater square platform visible from the surface in most commercial springs and sinks is a training platform where divers can congregate on the bottom without stirring up sediments and clouding the water. Free of waves and turbidity, but with depth and water clarity, Florida's springs are the best diver training areas available, attracting classes from around the Southeast.
Cypress Spring, Washington County

THE SPRINGS OF FLORIDA

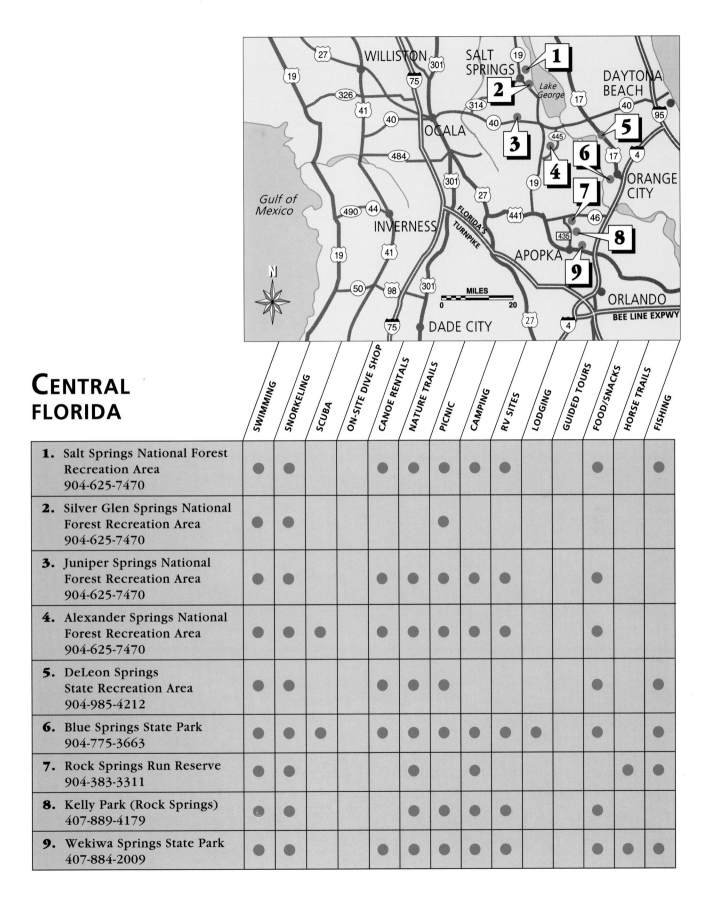

CENTRAL FLORIDA

	SWIMMING	SNORKELING	SCUBA	ON-SITE DIVE SHOP	CANOE RENTALS	NATURE TRAILS	PICNIC	CAMPING	RV SITES	LODGING	GUIDED TOURS	FOOD/SNACKS	HORSE TRAILS	FISHING
1. Salt Springs National Forest Recreation Area 904-625-7470	•	•			•	•	•	•	•			•		•
2. Silver Glen Springs National Forest Recreation Area 904-625-7470	•	•					•							
3. Juniper Springs National Forest Recreation Area 904-625-7470	•	•			•	•	•	•	•			•		
4. Alexander Springs National Forest Recreation Area 904-625-7470	•	•	•		•	•	•	•	•			•		
5. DeLeon Springs State Recreation Area 904-985-4212	•	•			•	•	•					•		•
6. Blue Springs State Park 904-775-3663	•	•	•		•	•	•	•	•	•		•		
7. Rock Springs Run Reserve 904-383-3311	•	•				•		•					•	•
8. Kelly Park (Rock Springs) 407-889-4179	•	•				•	•	•	•			•		
9. Wekiwa Springs State Park 407-884-2009	•	•			•	•	•	•	•			•	•	•

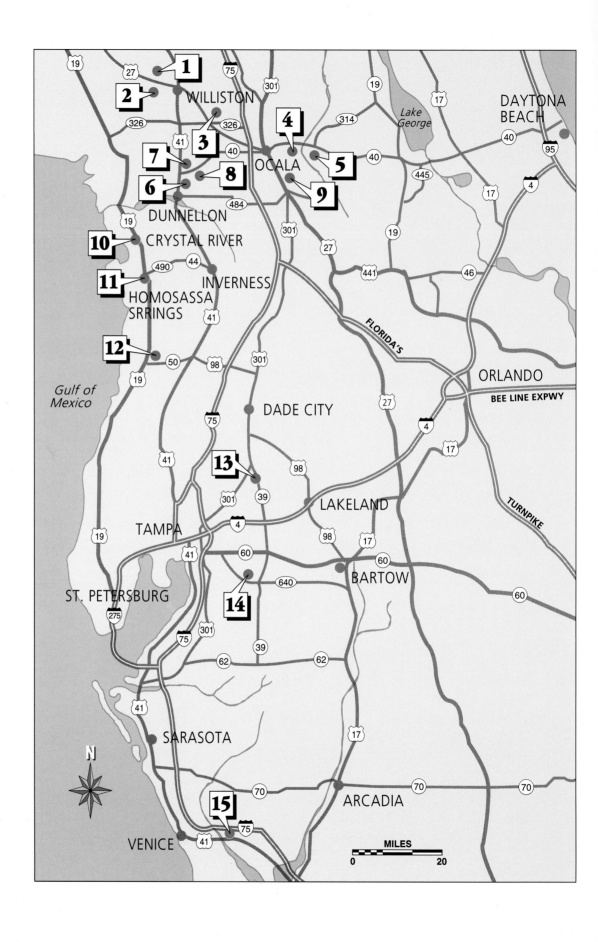

WEST AND SOUTH CENTRAL FLORIDA

	SWIMMING	SNORKELING	SCUBA	ON-SITE DIVE SHOP	CANOE RENTALS	NATURE TRAILS	PICNIC	CAMPING	RV SITES	LODGING	GUIDED TOURS	FOOD/SNACKS	HORSE TRAILS	FISHING
1. Devils Den 904-528-3344	●	●	●	●		●	●	●	●			●	●	
2. Blue Grotto 904-528-5770	●	●	●	●			●	●	●			●		
3. Forty Fathom Grotto 407-896-4541			●	●										
4. Silver Springs 800-274-7458						●					●	●		
5. Silver River State Park 904-466-3397	NOT YET OPEN													
6. KP Hole County Park 904-489-3055	●	●	●		●		●					●		●
7. Rainbow Springs State Park 904-489-8503						●	●							
8. Rainbow River State Campground 904-489-5201	●	●	●		●		●	●	●			●		●
9. Paradise Spring 904-368-5746			●				●							
10. Crystal River National Wildlife Refuge 904-563-2088	●	●	●	●	●					●	●	●		●
11. Homosassa Springs State Wildlife Park 904-628-2311						●	●				●	●		
12. Weeki Wachee Springs 800-678-9395	●										●	●		
13. Crystal Springs Park 813-782-5218	●	●	●		●	●	●					●		
14. Lithia Springs County Park 813-744-5572	●	●					●	●	●					●
15. Warm Mineral Springs Resort & Spa 813-426-1692	●	●								●		●		

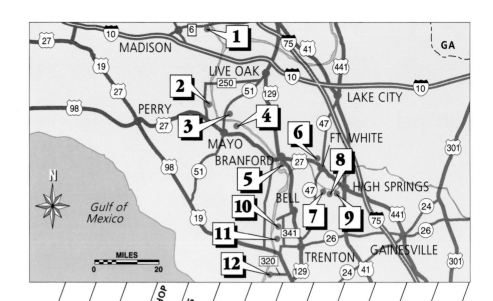

NORTH CENTRAL FLORIDA

	Swimming	Snorkeling	Scuba	On-Site Dive Shop	Canoe Rentals	Nature Trails	Picnic	Camping	RV Sites	Lodging	Guided Tours	Food/Snacks	Horse Trails	Fishing
1. Madison Blue Springs Resort 904-971-2880	●	●	●	●		●	●	●				●	●	●
2. Mayo Blue Springs Park 904-294-1617	●	●			●	●	●	●				●		●
3. Peacock Springs State Recreation Area 904-497-2511	●	●	●			●								●
4. River Rendezvous-Convict Spring 800-533-5276	●	●	●	●	●		●	●	●	●	●			●
5. Branford Spring Park No phone	●	●	●	●			●			●		●		●
6. Ichetucknee Springs State Park 904-497-2511	●	●	●		●	●	●					●		
7. Ginnie Springs Resort 800-874-8571	●	●	●	●	●	●	●	●	●					●
8. Blue Springs Park 904-454-1369	●	●				●	●	●				●		●
9. Poe Springs Park 904-454-1992	●	●			●	●	●					●		●
10. Hart Spring County Park 904-463-6486	●	●			●	●	●					●		●
11. Otter Springs RV Resort 904-463-2696	●	●	●		●	●	●	●	●			●	●	●
12. Manatee Springs State Park 904-493-6072	●	●	●		●	●	●	●	●	●	●	●		●

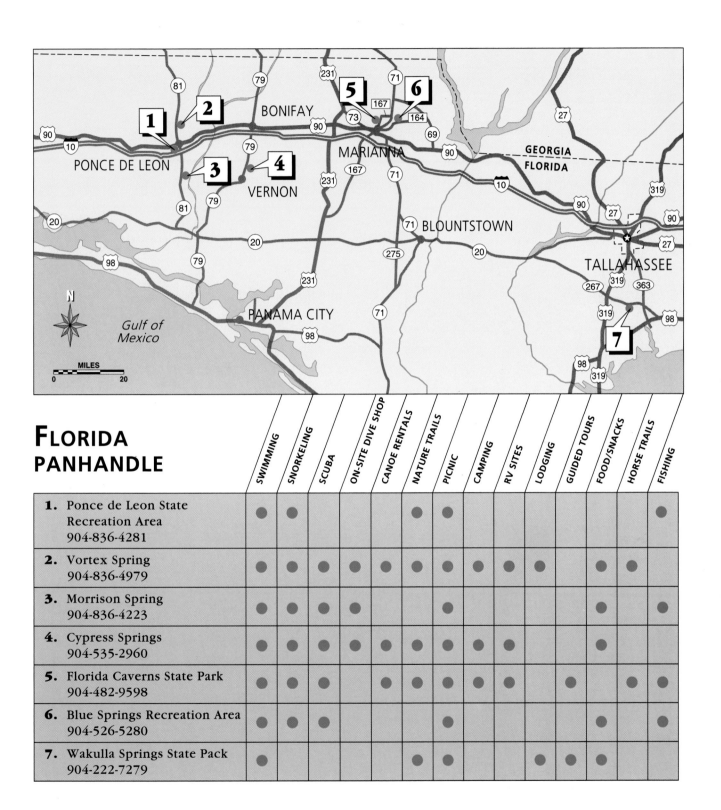

FLORIDA PANHANDLE

	SWIMMING	SNORKELING	SCUBA	ON-SITE DIVE SHOP	CANOE RENTALS	NATURE TRAILS	PICNIC	CAMPING	RV SITES	LODGING	GUIDED TOURS	FOOD/SNACKS	HORSE TRAILS	FISHING
1. Ponce de Leon State Recreation Area 904-836-4281	●	●				●	●							●
2. Vortex Spring 904-836-4979	●	●	●	●	●	●	●	●	●	●		●	●	
3. Morrison Spring 904-836-4223	●	●	●	●			●					●		●
4. Cypress Springs 904-535-2960	●	●	●	●	●	●	●	●	●			●		
5. Florida Caverns State Park 904-482-9598	●	●				●	●	●	●		●		●	●
6. Blue Springs Recreation Area 904-526-5280	●	●	●				●					●		●
7. Wakulla Springs State Pack 904-222-7279	●					●	●			●	●	●		

CHAPTER 7

Wild Springs

"... we set off in the cool of the morning, and descended pleasantly, riding on the crystal flood, which flows down with an easy, gentle, yet active current, rolling over its silvery bed; how abundantly are the waters replenished with inhabitants: the stream almost as transparent as the air we breathe; there is nothing done in secret except on its green flowery verges, where nature at the hand of the Supreme Creator, hath spread a mantle. . . ."

William Bartram, 1775

Seen from an underwater perspective, canoers gliding over the surface of Florida's spring rivers and streams will travel an ancient journey that reveals an abundance of life above and below the water.

Although many of Florida's springs are most visibly tourist attractions, campgrounds and park areas, and advertisements for them abound, the great majority of springs are still wild. Some rise up in remote abundance at the edge of Florida rivers, while others form blue pools in distant regions of forest. There are many springs along many canoe trails, back roads and sandy paths that must be searched for to find.

From its source in Georgia to its mouth in the Gulf of Mexico, the Suwannee River travels a winding course for over 200 miles across Florida. Along its way more than 20 spring sites add to its flow. The 80-mile course of the Chipola River from Alabama to its confluence with the Apalachicola River also is fed by many springs along its way.

The Santa Fe River's meandering journey to the Suwannee through mostly scenic forest is fed by dozens of wild springs including the Ichetucknee River, itself a pure spring river with many springs along its stream. Add to those the Wacissa, Wekiwa and Juniper, all pure spring rivers containing more springs in some of Florida's most wild regions. And at the end of sandy back roads we can find Saw Grass, Chassahowitzka and Nichols Springs.

These and many more springs we can find beneath our canoes and at the end of other roads. We can, without asking, swim in them on a hot summer's day. We can dive in them and view creatures from both fresh water and the sea. We can search spring sands for fossils of shells and teeth of sharks, bones of mastodon and sloth, arrowheads

A group of fossil hunters search a crack in limestone bedrock that can produce an abundance of fossil shells, teeth and bones from many periods in Florida's prehistory.

Fossilized shark teeth on a spring bottom, underwater treasure to diving fossil hunters, are preserved razor sharp after millions of years entombed in limestone. The larger center tooth is from an alligator probably of this century. The shark teeth are from creatures living at the time of Florida's creation, 600,000 centuries past.

The sleek shape of an approaching canoe and the spring it enters have changed little in form through the last few thousand years. Travelers on the surface above through coming ages will likely see the same wonder in these places as the many generations who have passed here before.

A canoer explores a wild spring rising through the bottom of a clear river near where it meets the Gulf. Canoers have especially good access to wilderness springs that occur within or flow into many Florida rivers.

and glass medicine bottles; relics that trace Florida's history — ancient and new.

Around these wild springs we can camp alone, build our fires, catch our food and spend our nights in these same spring places for the same reasons as those who traveled here centuries before. Here we watch wildlife undisturbed in its daily discourse and hear the sounds of secluded forests. These are springs protected by their wildness and by visitors who leave them as they always were. In the seeking

and finding of these wild places, we can perhaps best find in ourselves the traveler and explorer.

As Bartram found Florida's springs to be rare and special places in our world, so do we, and he would be pleased to know that in future centuries, protected and preserved in many ways and forms, the springs of Florida will continue their winding and wondrous course through the environment and minds of travelers to come.

APPENDIX A
MORE ABOUT SPRINGS INHABITANTS

This appendix contains further information about the life cycles, habitats, food and behavior of the springs inhabitants pictured in this book. Species are arranged alphabetically by common name.

ALLIGATOR

An alligator in the springs environment is not an unusual occurrence, especially in large spring rivers and isolated springs. In those springs where they are present, they move about with assurance and authority.

The alligator (*Alligator mississippiensis*) resides at the very top of the food chain. Once it has gained lengths to three feet, having avoided gar, raccoons, herons, and other alligators, it has no natural enemies. The alligator, on the other hand, is a natural enemy to virtually any smaller creature that ventures into its path.

The alligator is well equipped as an aquatic predator. Specially developed eyes and nostrils that barely protrude above the water allow a gradual approach to prey. When its prey is near, it opens its mouth and, with a quick sideways thrust, grasps its prey in powerful jaws. Large prey is pulled into the water and thrashed and rolled violently until the prey is drowned or too stunned to resist. Pigs, dogs, cattle, deer, beaver, muskrat, egrets, turtles and fish are all potential victims of the alligator.

Alligators are primarily nocturnal creatures, spending their days basking in the sun or resting in warm water. At night they hunt. Their periscopelike eyes hold pupils that contract to vertical slits in bright light, but at night expand to nearly fill the eye. When exposed to a light at night, the eyes reflect a brilliant red.

The Spanish, upon arriving in Florida, named the alligator "el lagarto" — the lizard. The similarities they share with the lizard do not end in appearance. Alligators are astonishingly swift creatures on land as well as in the water. Their powerful tail encompasses half their length and propels them through water with ease. Their normally slow movements on land are deceiving. They can, if threatened or when attacking prey, rise up on their legs and run with tremendous speed.

Breeding occurs from April to June with the female taking the initiative. The male is content to doze peacefully in shallow water and warm sun, all the while emitting a pungent, musky odor from musk glands located beneath his lower jaw. The female searches him out and, after finding him, seduces him by slithering over his body, grunting and blowing bubbles under his chin. Once enticed, he completes their ritual underwater.

The female then gathers bark, grasses, twigs and leaves to build a nest. She heaps her gatherings into a mound two or more feet high and up to four feet wide. By June or July she has laid anywhere from 15 to 75 white eggs in the nest and covers them with mud and debris to be warmed by the sun and decaying vegetation. Her first duties completed, she retires to her den to keep a watchful eye over the nest. She is most dangerous during this period, and any animal or human who should approach too near her nest is subject to attack.

The eggs hatch in about two months with the young grunting as they emerge, signalling the watchful mother to uncover the nest. The sex of the young is determined by nest temperature during incubation. The warmer the nest, the greater the number of males. Their mother guards them until the following spring when the survivors of her brood will be 16 inches long. She then abandons them to fend alone.

Adult male alligators are estimated to live up to 50 years, and lengths may reach 19 feet. Females are the smaller sex and rarely exceed ten feet in length. Any alligator longer than ten feet is likely to be a male. Breeding for both sexes begins when lengths reach five feet and ages reach six to ten years.

The alligator is a potentially dangerous animal. A blow from its tail can break a human leg, and, although extremely rare, attacks on humans in the water occur. Alligators are by nature reclusive creatures, avoiding human contact. Those alligators fed handouts, and that lose their fear of humans, are the most dangerous.

Alligators occur in only two regions of the world. The American alligator is present from North Carolina south to southern Florida and along the coastal states to Texas. A close relative of the American species, the Chinese alligator, inhabits the waters of the Yangtze River.

AMERICAN EEL

Eels in the springs environment are primarily cave dwellers, but many inhabit dark niches found in beds of vegetation, beneath rocks and in cracks and crevices in limestone walls. They are common residents of all Florida rivers and lakes that have access to the sea and are one of the most widely distributed spring inhabitants. Panhandle springs have especially abundant populations.

Eels (*Auguilla rostrata*) are one of the most common transient residents of the cave environment, inhabiting almost all of Florida's springs. Rarely seen by day, they reside in dark niches or burrow into sand until night. Then, as voracious carnivores, they leave their caves at dusk to feed on smaller fish, insects and crayfish. Eels have an additional advantage as predators — a rare ability to leave the water and crawl snakelike through moist areas while searching land prey or while migrating.

American eels have been found from Greenland south to Bermuda, central and northern South America and far into the interior of North America in rivers and their tributaries that flow into the Atlantic Ocean and Gulf of Mexico. Their European counterparts are commercially fished and considered a delicacy when jellied, cooked in olive oil or smoked. In North America, eels are an excellent but neglected food source. The skins of American eels were once used in the production of quality book bindings and riding and buggy whips.

Of all spring inhabitants none must accomplish a more distant and perilous journey to eventually reside in this environment. Eels are born in the Sargasso Sea, a region of the North Atlantic east of the Bahamas and southwest of Bermuda. Their initial appearance from the depths of Sargasso is as transparent "leptocephalus" or glass eels, resembling a leaf more than an eel. Except for conspicuous eyes, they are almost invisible in the water. From the Sargasso they swim and drift near the surface for a year, growing slowly as they gradually approach land. When they reach the North American coast in the spring of the year, they undergo a relatively rapid metamorphosis and become "elvers," resembling adult eels but with lengths rarely exceeding 3 1/2 inches.

The young female elvers that survive the first leg of their migration are ready to swim up rivers from Canada through the Gulf States to spend most of their lives in fresh water. The males will usually remain near a river's mouth. In Florida, female eels inhabit springs for 8 to 12 years, reaching lengths of more than 50 inches. Waiting males in the Gulf and Atlantic rarely attain lengths of more than 24 inches. Eels have few enemies once they reach fresh water and spend their lives in the springs in preparation for a return pilgrimage to the Sargasso.

At the end of their sojourn in the springs, in anticipation of their final migration, eels begin to mature sexually, undergoing another fascinating transformation that pervades their entire body. Internally, their sexual organs develop, their digestive tract diminishes, thyroid and pituitary glands become more active, and special cells designed to rid their bodies of excess oceanic salts become more numerous in their gills. Externally, their dull yellow-green coloration becomes a silver metallic sheen, and their backs turn a dark purplish black. The skin thickens and toughens as scales become securely fixed. Nostrils dilate, and their lateral-line sense organs increase in size along their sides. Eyes change dramatically, doubling in size. The retina quadruples in size, and total eye volume increases eightfold. The eye pigment of the retina changes from purple, which is most sensitive to the blue-green light characteristic of fresh water, to a gold hue, which is most receptive to the blue wavelengths of light that penetrate deepest in ocean depths. The "silver eels" that result no longer feed and, in their transformation, have changed from nocturnal freshwater inhabitants to deep-sea fishes.

Finally, in the fall of the year in conjunction with the dark phases of the moon, their migration begins. The females join the males and together swim by the millions, probably guided by a sensitivity to the earth's magnetic field and orientation to night stars. During their return journey, many again fall prey to a variety of marine fishes. The survivors that arrive from all over North America, and their European relatives that have traveled longer and farther, congregate once more in the depths of the Sargasso Sea. After their unknown rituals of spawning have been completed, the adults are not seen again. In the dark depths of the Sargasso where they were spawned, it is assumed they also die.

AMERICAN SHAD

The oceanic American shad (*Alosa sapidissima*) are not common spring residents in Florida and occur primarily in large springs that ultimately flow into the Atlantic Ocean via the St. Johns River. They ascend fresh waters in spring to spawn where their eggs are strewn into the current and abandoned. The fry drift downstream to enter the ocean in the fall. Little is known of their life in the sea. After five years in oceanic waters, they return again to fresh water as adults to spawn.

The American shad originally was found only on the eastern coasts of North America but, through introductions, now is established on western shores from California to Alaska. An esteemed food and gamefish in some parts of the eastern United States, it is caught by fly fishing and trolling. Its scientific name, *Alosa sapidissima*, means "shad-most delicious."

APPLE SNAIL

The apple snail (*Pomacea paludosa*) is common to most of Florida's lakes, rivers and springs. In springs it is most abundant in slow currents and headsprings or in the calm eddies and niches of swifter runs. With feeble eyes and probing antennae, it moves about with muscular contractions of its foot, leaving in its path a shiny secretion of lubricant that assists it in sliding along at a pace typical of a snail. Oxygen is obtained through a specialized dual system — gills for use underwater and an extendable snorkellike siphon or tube, visible just below the shell, for breathing air when it floats at the surface or leaves the water.

The apple snail roams mainly at night, feeding on algae and plants with a sharp, rasping tongue capable of devouring all but the toughest aquatic vegetation. When populations become overabundant in localized areas, these voracious snails can overgraze a luxuriant spring to near barren sand.

During warmer months, apple snails emerge at night from the water to lay their eggs on stumps, logs, dock posts, grass blades or whatever objects will hold a snail's weight. After incubating for a number of weeks, the miniature apple snails hatch and fall into the water.

Excavations of prehistoric villages and camps reveal that the apple snail was once used as a plentiful source of human food. Apple snails, to a small degree, are still eaten today.

ATLANTIC NEEDLEFISH

Needlefish (*Strongylura marina*) in springs are endlessly on the move and most often visible traveling in pairs or small groups just beneath the surface. They are impressive fishes and masters of life at the water's surface. Needlefish are designed like arrows, with fins oppositely placed toward the rear making them extremely swift and accurate in their fearsome attacks on smaller fishes. They are exceptionally maneuverable fishes even at high speed. Their coloration of dark backs and silvery sides and undersides acts as camouflage, making them almost undiscernible near the surface.

The Atlantic needlefish range near shore in oceanic waters from Massachusetts south along the coast to Brazil. Greenish-colored bones tend to discourage their utilization as a food fish throughout their range, although their flesh is of exceptional quality.

A needlefish's similarities to an arrow do not stop at appearance. It has a skittish and unpredictable reaction to being in the spotlight of a diver's light at night. Attempts at close-range night photography of needlefish often result in numerous collisions with a darting, bolting subject. One needlefish impacted against the photographer's light with alarming intent and with such force that its beak was left bent and broken in the ricochet.

BLACKBANDED DARTER

The blackbanded darter (*Percina nigrofasciata*), by its larger size, is the more visibly abundant of the two darters common to Florida's springs. Their habits of darting about the bottom and coming to rest on their pectoral fins are distinctive characteristics of the bottom-dwelling darters. In exceptionally swift waters these darters avoid the current by hiding on the down-current side of rocks and logs or in cracks in limestone outcrops.

The range of the blackbanded darter extends to the coastal streams of the southeast from South Carolina to Louisiana. This and other darter species are close relatives of the perch and walleye of more northern waters.

BLACK CRAPPIE

The black crappie (*Pomoxis nigromaculatus*) of Florida's springs is generally a timid and reclusive species not eager to allow the approach of divers. Not likely to be seen at all from the surface, when discovered underwater, they most often huddle in small groups beneath docks, rock overhangs and floating vegetation. In their preferred habitat of warm, shallow lakes, they are found in large schooling groups.

Like other members of their family, male crappies are nest builders and attract several females to their nests fanned in the bottom. The male remains to guard the eggs from marauding bream and stays with the fry until they disperse a few days after hatching. Crappies are notably graceful fishes as they maneuver with large dorsal and anal fins of equal size.

BLUE CRAB

The profusion of blue crabs (*Callinectes sapidus*) in Florida's fresh water is in part due to their mode of reproduction. Two major migrations occur in the lives of blue crabs — one when the young of both sexes swim upstream, and the other when impregnated females swim downstream.

In the autumn of each year, a female in fresh water undergoes a molt, becomes soft-shelled and begins mating. Her hard-shelled mate will carry and protect her beneath his body as they lock in an embrace lasting almost a week. After their lengthy ritual, the female leaves fresh water and swims downstream to saline waters to wait out winter hibernation. As waters warm in spring, the adult and young crabs emerge and her young begin their first journey upstream.

Blue crabs are excellent swimmers, well streamlined for their style of sideways swimming. Propelled by walking legs modified to serve as paddles, their swimming migrations may take them more then ten miles a day to distances of more than a hundred miles from their estuaries. The muscles that propel a blue crab, whose scientific name means "beautiful and tasty swimmer," are what make it an important commercial seafood species despite its relatively small size.

The nocturnal blue crabs, when present in springs, tend to displace freshwater crayfish and take over the role of spring scavengers. In addition to eating carrion, they are also efficient predators. They can jump from the bottom with amazing speed to grasp passing fish with their sharp pincers. Attempts by divers to capture a blue crab can result in bleeding wounds to hands and fingers from pincers also well designed for defense.

BLUEGILL

Bluegills (*Lepomis machrochirus mystacalis*) are one of Florida's most abundant freshwater fishes. They are not a true schooling species but do maintain loose aggregations as they move about. Larger adults roam freely in springs and frequently are the fish most likely to be tamed by offerings of bread

tossed on the water. Young bluegills are more reclusive and rarely leave the cover of vegetation.

The bluegills' spawning season extends from early spring to late fall but is most intense in spring with great numbers of bluegills gathering in sandy shallows to build their nests in spawning colonies. The male fans a small depression in the sand and, with his colors heightened, swims proudly around his nest waiting to impress a passing female. Nests are often within 12 inches of one another, making competition and nest protection a constant routine of confronting neighboring males and routing intruders.

Once a female has entered a male's nest, and after proper courting, they swim on their sides together as they spawn. After depositing her eggs, she quickly leaves to find another male and spawn again. The male will remain to guard the eggs until they hatch and then guard the fry until they are able to leave the nest.

A variety of smaller creatures are prey to the bluegill, but insects and their larvae are preferred. Vegetation often supplements their diet. Smaller bluegills are, in turn, favorite prey to the basses.

The bluegill is common to lakes, rivers and springs throughout the eastern United States and is one of Florida's most popular sporting sunfishes.

BLUE TILAPIA

The blue tilapia's presence in Florida dates from 1961, when experimental tilapia were introduced to phosphate mining pits in Hillsborough County. Under controlled conditions, the tilapia was being studied for its potential as a noncompetitive, edible and "catchable" sportfish that, as a plant-eater, had potential merits as an agent in aquatic weed control. Before the study was completed (which determined that blue tilapia would not be a desirable addition to Florida waters), tilapia were illegally taken from the control ponds and stocked in private ponds and public lakes. As a result, by 1968, the blue tilapia was described as one of the fastest-spreading exotics in Florida.

Blue tilapia (*Tilapia aurea*) are generally confined to the south-central regions of the state, but their range is gradually extending northward. The cooler winter waters of north Florida have limited their expansion, but their introduction to the warmer waters of northern springs could enhance their proliferation and lead to potentially unfortunate consequences for springs and their inhabitants.

The tilapia's success in invading Florida waters is partially due to its proficiency in the art of reproduction. After the eggs are laid, the mouthbrooding tilapia holds the eggs inside its mouth for better protection. Later, when danger threatens the fry, the guarding adult opens its mouth, and the fry stream inside for safety. Tilapia lay relatively few eggs, but 14 tilapia can produce 14,000 young in ten weeks.

The blue tilapia has not become the sportfish it was hoped to be. They rarely bite a baited hook, preferring algae instead. Their excellent edibility has, however, inspired a commercial and private net fishery that is beginning to utilize and help control the tilapia. Commonly misnamed the "Nile bream" or "Nile perch," the blue tilapia remains an unwelcome inhabitant of Florida's southern springs, lakes and rivers.

BOWFIN

The bowfin (*Amia calva*) is common to all Florida fresh waters but prefers rivers and lakes to the more visible environments of springs.

Like gars, bowfins are survivors of an otherwise extinct order of fishes, but unlike the gars they constitute the sole living species of their group. Their ancient origins are evident in their bony scales and the sheath of bony plates that covers their semicartilaginous skull. Well armed with pointed teeth, the bowfins prey on whatever smaller creatures are available or vulnerable.

Bowfins are found in North America from the Mississippi River basin eastward. They are an extremely hardy fish within their range, due in part to the air-breathing ability they share with gars, which enables them to live in waters uninhabitable by most other fishes.

The tenacity of the bowfin has been recorded in remarkable incidents. A bowfin accidently left in an aquarium without food was discovered a year later still alive, though thinned by the experience. Another was found aestivating four inches deep in moist soil, stranded a quarter mile from a river that had flooded and receded. Occasionally, adult bowfins are discovered living successfully with no eyes.

BROWN DARTER

Brown darters abound in many headspring environments and runs where vegetation affords them cover and currents keep their water clear. Both their coloration and size make the brown darter one of the least-known inhabitants of the springs.

The brown darter (*Etheostoma edwini*) rarely seems to be brown in the springs environment. The female displays the typical light green of her sex with a black band across her eye. The male retains the black band and displays numerous small red dots on his sides. Spawning occurs year-round for the darters, and the male's spots tend to brighten as he courts the female with prancing motions and fin display.

Brown darters are bottom dwellers, moving across the bottom with the short hops and darts that have given them their name. They rest on their pectoral fins with heads erect, in constant view of their surroundings. The darters are quick to prey on plankton and whatever insects, worms and larvae their small size allows. Should the need arise, they can swim with impressive speed into deeper cover to avoid the many larger fishes that seek them out.

Like many springs inhabitants, the brown darter is restricted in range to clear, vegetated streams of southeastern Alabama, northern Florida, and southern Georgia.

CAVE CRAYFISH

Troglobitic crayfish (*Procambarus horsti*) in Florida represent an especially abundant and unique group of true cave dwellers. In addition to the severe adaptations of blindness and lack of pigmentation, their food requirement is relatively small, as is the amount of energy they expend. They move slowly, their endurance when swimming is low, and their bodies are unarmored and more delicate in comparison to their relatives at the surface. There is some evidence their adaptations allow for a life span in excess of 100 years.

Cave crayfish live a seemingly difficult and fragile existence. Their most difficult task is obtaining food in a barren environment. With no visual cues to seek food, they move calmly about their domain, stopping often as they flick their short, chemosensitive antennae, adept at detecting the presence of food. When food is detected, they move slowly, exploring their immediate surroundings by sweeping their long touch-sensitive antennae from side to side until their food is found. Like all crayfish, they are additionally aided by their pincered feet equipped to detect food by taste.

Although crayfish are capable of eating almost anything organic, cave crayfish are additionally limited to what little food filters down into caves. Occasionally they will move near or into the open spring if small cracks and fissures give them access to the surface. Recent studies indicate crayfish populations are extremely small or nonexistent in areas where clay overlies cave systems and prevents the movement of organic material into the aquifer. Movement from their caves, however, presents its own danger. Their color, slow movements and lack of sight make them particularly vulnerable to predation. Though unable to detect night or day by sight, they retain the nocturnal activity patterns of surface crayfish. With night, most surface predators are inactive and movement to the surface by cave crayfish is a somewhat safer venture.

As difficult an environment as it may be, Florida's spring caves contain the most diverse populations of troglobitic crayfish in the world. Contributing most to their unusual diversity are the large numbers of springs present and the availability of food to move into the aquifer. In some areas, spring caves less than one kilometer apart are inhabited by different species of crayfish. In other areas, a species may inhabit a large system of interconnected spring caves.

CHAIN PICKEREL

Members of the pickerel family are notorious as predacious carnivores, and chain pickerel (*Esox niger*) are no exception. Pickerel primarily attack fishes but will take almost anything alive and small enough to be swallowed. Pickerel have been observed taking fish half their size and digesting the front of their prey as the tail and body protrude from their mouths.

Chain pickerel are highly successful in their pursuit of food. They hover quietly, well camouflaged, waiting for prey to move near, then suddenly bolt with tremendous speed to catch the passerby. They will also stalk slowly through vegetation, barely moving as they intently search ahead for an unsuspecting meal.

The chain pickerel spawn in late winter and spring. No nest preparations are made. A female and one or two males swim over vegetation releasing eggs and milt and then disperse the eggs with violent lashes of their tails. The abandoned eggs

hatch in a week, and the fry attach themselves to bottom vegetation with an adhesive snout.

Those fry that elude the many fishes that prey on them will grow to an average of two feet in length and may reach ages of nine years. The largest known chain pickerel also claimed the angling record. A chain pickerel caught in Homerville, Georgia, in 1961 was 31 inches long and weighed nine pounds, six ounces.

The chain pickerel ranges from southeastern Canada south along the Atlantic states to central Florida, and west to east Texas. Despite its relatively small size, the chain pickerel is a popular and fighting gamefish throughout its range.

CREVALLE JACK

Crevalle jacks (*Caranx hippos*) are most abundant in springs primarily in winter when they enter in large wandering schools. Jacks are incredibly swift fishes and look the part in their ability to decimate schools of their prey. Their stay in fresh water is relatively short, either because their tolerance for it is low or because their food supply is insufficient to maintain their stay. An extended stay by jacks could have serious consequences on the populations of smaller springs inhabitants.

Crevalle jacks are famous worldwide for their tenacity as a gamefish. They may weigh over 40 pounds and require hours to land on light tackle. Small jacks are savage fighters and put up a surprising battle for their size. Their flesh is not highly valued in the United States, but in Central America, jacks are highly prized as a food fish. The larger the jack, however, the less palatable its flesh becomes.

Crevalle jacks are part of a large family and the most common species of the family to invade fresh water. The reflective silver coloration and light yellow tinge above the lateral line on the crevalle jack make it distinguishable from its many relatives. Jacks inhabit tropical and temperate seas around the world.

FLIER

Fliers (*Centrarchus macropterns*) appear to be a very rare inhabitant of Florida's springs and are included here because, in the one spring where they were found by the author, they were the only fish species visibly present, occupying Otter Springs with a population in the hundreds. There, they were found only in the crevice that dominates the small headspring pool and at the cave mouth 25 feet below.

Fliers are a sunfish species more common to dark water bayous, swamps and tannic rivers, where their high tolerance for acidic water allows them to thrive where no other sunfish species could survive. The population in Otter Springs is probably the result of the nearby Suwannee River flooding over the spring and leaving the fliers to dominate the small pool. An identifiable characteristic of these brown fishes is their dorsal and anal fins, which, like the crappie, are almost identical in size. Many rows of spots run down their sides.

Fliers are a southern species, found from Virginia across the Gulf States and up the Mississippi River as far as Illinois. In Florida, fliers range the north and central regions where most of the state's dark water rivers are found.

FLORIDA GAR

Florida gars (*Lepisosteus platrhynchus*) are timid creatures, often congregating in large groups like their relatives but preferring the security of vegetative cover to moving about in open water as the longnose. Smaller springs that flow into rivers frequently attract congregations of these gars at the spring's mouth. Occasionally, they move up runs at night in search of prey. The Florida gars are no less voracious than their larger counterparts, but their size limits their prey primarily to smaller fishes.

The Florida gar has one nearly identical relative present in Florida. The spotted gar, *Lepisosteus oculatus*, dwells in the panhandle west of the Ochlockonee River. The bony scales on the throat of the spotted gar distinguish it from the Florida gar, which has no throat scales. Both of these species rarely attain lengths greater than two feet. In comparison to most freshwater fishes, the Florida gar is a relatively rare species with a limited range. It is restricted to fresh waters extending from the southern tip of peninsular Florida northward into the lowlands of Georgia and westward to the Ochlockonee River.

FLORIDA LARGEMOUTH BASS

The Florida largemouth bass (*Micropterus salmoides floridanus*) ranks among the few dominant predators of the springs environment as well as of fresh waters throughout the peninsula. As a spring inhabitant, it resides in the quieter and more vegetated waters of headsprings and slow-moving rivers. The larger individuals move through their domain choosing their course and habitat with little fear of predation. Largemouth bass are the primary predators here and take whatever smaller creatures their size will allow.

They are fierce hunters. Few fishes can match their power and speed as they lunge from dense vegetation in camouflage to engulf their unsuspecting prey. Smaller fishes comprise most of their diet, but they commonly take frogs, mice, crayfish, birds, snakes, eels and turtles. Juvenile largemouth bass prefer the easier prey of minnows, insects, worms, and snails.

For the largemouth bass, spawning begins as early as December and proceeds into summer. The males become aggressive and territorial as they select a spawning site and sweep it clean. Males vigorously defend the resulting small, circular area from all passersby. The male patiently awaits the arrival of receptive females, attracting them with a display of swimming acrobatics. An interested female enters the nest, and after tender biting and nipping, they deposit eggs and milt. Her eggs only partially spent, the female moves on to find another suitor. But for the male, the duties of reproduction have only just begun.

The male will stay to fan and protect the eggs from constant intrusions by numerous predators. The eggs hatch in less than a week, and the male must then begin the more difficult task of guarding the nomadic, schooling fry. While the schooling fry travel randomly about their waters, they are repeatedly attacked by sunfishes that take fry on each pass of the school. As the male fends off an attack from one side, another predator sweeps through the school from another side. Relatively few members of a school survive.

Those largemouth bass that reach adult size in Florida and in Georgia will become the largest of their species in the world. Warm waters and plentiful food encourage record sizes and ages. Adult largemouth bass in Florida will attain weights up to 20 pounds and ages of more than 15 years. The world-record largemouth bass, caught in Georgia in 1932, weighed 22.25 pounds.

FLORIDA SNAPPING TURTLE

Florida snapping turtles (*Chelydra osceola*) are largely nocturnal, omnivorous creatures with an appetite for almost any creature, dead or alive. Plants, apple snails, crayfish, mammals, water snakes, waterfowl and numerous other birds comprise their diet. Snappers wait in ambush for much of their prey and strike out with jaws agape when a victim comes into range of their long necks. Periodically they seek out their victims. Waterfowl occasionally are approached slowly from beneath the water and then suddenly grabbed and pulled under. Larger mammals taken at the water's edge are caught in a crushing bite, then dragged into the water and held until they drown.

Female snappers leave the water in May and June to lay their eggs in small depressions dug in soft ground or sand. The hatchling snappers emerge from their nest in late summer and immediately head for water. Adult snappers on land are potentially dangerous turtles if approached too near. Few turtles are as ill-tempered. A confrontation will typically cause a snapper to rise high up on its legs and lunge repeatedly with snapping jaws. Once it bites and has hold, it is not easily removed.

Florida snapping turtles are restricted to peninsular Florida with populations greatest in the Everglades. Almost any body of water, however, is a potential home for these sturdy turtles. Although droughts will kill many, when water is scarce snappers have been reported to bury themselves in mud for weeks with no apparent harm.

The Florida snapper differs slightly from the more common snapper that inhabits almost all of North America. The Florida snapper has numerous tubercles about its head and neck, and occasionally dark stripes may appear across the face. The question as to whether the Florida snapper is a subspecies of the more common snapper, *Chelydra serpentina*, or a separate species has not been resolved.

The snapping turtle is a favored turtle for soups and stews in the northern limits of its range. The snapper in Florida is not as sought after in light of other numerous turtles considered to be of better quality.

FLORIDA SOFTSHELL TURTLE

The Florida softshell (*Trionyx ferox*) is a turtle of large springs, lakes and calm waters of rivers. Its fondness for burrowing in the bottom keeps some areas of its habitat too disturbed to develop plant growth. Areas of barren sand are likely spots to look for its periscoping head. Its fondness for the bottom is equally matched by its ability to quickly disappear and tunnel into it. Schools of fish are frequently seen hovering near a hidden softshell, waiting for food the turtle displaces from the sand.

Softshells are primarily aquatic turtles that rarely leave the water. They occasionally go to shore and bask in the sun, but only where they can very suddenly dash back to water. Unlike most turtles, the softshell can run on land with startling speed and ability.

Florida softshells are omnivorous turtles, but plants are not particularly favored. They tend to prefer feeding on insects, frogs, crayfish, fish, small waterfowl and carrion. Young softshells are vulnerable to a great number of predators. Adults need fear only the alligator.

After mating, a female softshell will leave the water in mid-March through July to dig a small nest in sandy soil exposed to the sun. After depositing an average of 20 eggs, she carefully covers the nest, moves away a few yards, and vigorously scratches the ground. Her conspicuous trace may serve to draw potential egg predators away from the actual nest. The eggs, if undisturbed, will hatch in two months.

Florida softshells are the heaviest and bulkiest of North American softshells but have the smallest geographic range. Adult females may reach two feet in width. Their dark brown-gray color may be mottled with white blotches around the face in older individuals. The males seldom exceed 12 inches in width. The Florida softshell occurs only from South Carolina south to Florida.

FRESHWATER SHRIMP

The freshwater shrimp (*Palaemonetes paludosus*) is a small, rarely noticed creature. It remains hidden by day among the tangles of vegetation and algae where its transparent body and one-inch size make it nearly invisible to its many predators. It waits until night to venture about and feed on microscopic plankton.

The freshwater variety of shrimp closely resembles the much larger saltwater species in both form and locomotion. Forward movement is most frequently used as it navigates in close quarters among vegetation. However, should a rapid flight be required, its powerful tail can propel it swiftly backwards.

A shrimp is normally transparent within the clear water of springs, but has developed, to a striking degree, an ability to blend with its background. The freshwater shrimp is equipped with four types of pigment granules — white, red, yellow and blue. By changing the relative dispersion and combination of the granules, the shrimp can fade into its surroundings with perfectly matched camouflage.

This species of freshwater shrimp is restricted to southern fresh waters along the Atlantic coast. In other areas of the world where similar shrimp are found, they are prized food when collected by the thousands and eaten whole.

GOLDEN SHINER

Shiners (*Notemigonus crysoleucas*), like the redeye chubs, are a schooling species, moving as a unit about their domain. Their schools usually become smaller as the shiners increase in size. As a schooling unit, the small shiners offer no particular target to their many enemies and, if attacked, will dart randomly in all directions, regrouping after the predator has passed.

Shiners are present throughout Florida fresh waters, but in springs they primarily inhabit the larger, deeper springs and spring rivers. Their schooling behavior, color, and the red-tipped fins of the larger adults make them easily recognizable. The shiners are surface and midwater feeders, snapping small bits of plants and plankton, which they approach with graceful, arcing banks and dives.

Spawning season for the shiner extends from early spring to late fall. Shiners deposit their adhesive eggs over vegetation and abandon them. Surprisingly, they have been reported to deposit their eggs in largemouth bass nests actively guarded by male bass.

The golden shiner now ranges throughout the lakes and rivers of North America, due partly to its popularity as a baitfish. Shiners are cultivated in ponds to be sold as bait and as food for fish hatcheries raising largemouth bass and other gamefishes. They have both purposely and inadvertently been introduced to waters outside their original range of eastern North America.

GRAY SNAPPER

Gray snappers (*Lutjanus griseus*) do not penetrate inland springs of Florida to a major degree. But when present in the few coastal springs they will invade, they often do so in great numbers. Spectacular schools can be observed hovering in tight formation about a cave entrance or hiding within cave corridors.

Coloration of the gray snapper can vary and will quickly change. A prominent dark streak across the eye will come and go in a few moments. Schooling snappers generally carry the facial streak. Snappers hidden in caves lose their streaks and take on a reddish tint similar to their limestone surroundings.

The gray snapper is a common fish in Florida's shallow coastal waters. Its excellent food quality makes it a much-sought saltwater gamefish throughout its range. The gray snapper is an abundant inhabitant of the Atlantic from New England to Bermuda, south to Brazil and west into the Gulf of Mexico. Its frequent presence in mangrove sloughs has given rise to another of its common names — the mangrove snapper.

GREATER SIREN

The siren (*Siren lacertina*) is a rare spring inhabitant, occupying primarily other varieties of such shallow-water habitats as ditches, ponds, flooded fields, lakes and river backwaters. It emerges from its bottom cover at night to forage for crayfish, snails and worms.

Greater sirens, aside from being nocturnal, are extremely secretive and, except in underwater encounters, are almost never seen. They remain secluded in deep vegetation or beneath leaves and debris in spring rivers or pools, but periodic need for air brings them swimming eel-like to the surface.

Sirens are true amphibians and one of the few that, when mature, still maintain features of the larval stage. A siren lacks hind legs but has two small forelegs with four toes each that may provide some aid in movement. The external gills that often hide the presence of the forelegs remain through the life span of the siren, which may exceed 25 years. Adult sirens can reach lengths of over three feet.

Relatively little is known of the breeding habits of this reclusive creature. Fertilization of eggs is known to be external, and eggs are deposited singly or in small groups on underwater vegetation. Young sirens are reported, in places, to abound among the hanging roots of water hyacinth.

The adult siren is well adapted to an uncertain aquatic environment. Should the water dry up in the siren's habitat, it descends into the mud, and if that in turn dries over, the siren entombs itself in an inelastic, parchmentlike cocoon excreted through the skin that covers its entire body except the mouth. Protected from desiccation, it lies motionless, sometimes for months, waiting for coming rains.

The siren, for whatever reason, is named after the beautiful temptresses of mythology who lured ancient sailors and their ships to doom upon hidden shallows and reefs.

HOGCHOKER SOLE

Hogchoker soles (*Trinectes maculatus*) are abundant in Florida's springs in areas of clean sand, often congregating in headspring bottoms and swimming areas. With a few quick flaps of its body, a hogchoker easily descends into the sand with only mouth and eyes protruding. Here it waits for passing prey of insect larvae. As the prey approaches, it shoots water through the underside gill to vault from the sand and grab its meal.

The hogchoker, like other soles and flounders, hatches as a normal, vertically upright fish. As it matures, one eye migrates around the head to the other side and the fish begins to live on one side — in the hogchoker's case, the left side. The gills remain each to a side with one on top and the other beneath.

An adult hogchoker may reach six inches in length, but adults are not found in fresh water. Only the young make the rigorous journey, often swimming hundreds of miles up rivers to eventually reside in springs. There, hogchokers are generally less than three inches long.

Immature hogchokers reside in springs throughout the year. As they grow larger and mature, they return to the sea to spawn and complete their life as an adult. Hogchokers range the waters of the Atlantic coast south to the Gulf coast of Florida. The explanation for their unflattering common name is a matter of conjecture.

LAKE CHUBSUCKER

Chubsuckers (*Erimyzon sucetta*) are graceful spring fishes adept at their role as nomadic wanderers. They roam large springs and their rivers in pairs or small groups, intermittently coasting and darting in spurts, propelled by quick tail thrusts.

The chubsuckers owe their name to their membership in the sucker family and, like the spotted suckers, they forage on the spring bottom. When feeding, they hover over a spot likely to contain bottom organisms and ingest mouthfuls of sand, filtering out great quantities of debris.

Chubsuckers are common residents of springs,

as well as rivers and lakes, which provide dense vegetation and ample room for their wanderings. Their range is extensive, including rivers and lakes from southern Wisconsin east to New England and south to Florida and Texas. What may be the largest chubsucker on record, weighing two pounds and measuring 15.2 inches long, was caught in Silver Springs.

LEAST KILLIFISH

Least killifish (*Heterandria formosa*) are members of the livebearer family along with their close relatives, the mosquitofish. Least killifish occupy the same type of habitat as mosquitofish, hiding near the surface in dense beds and mats of vegetation, but they are much less active in their movement within this cover. They swim in small concentrations, venturing inches at a time along branches or limestone walls searching for their microscopic prey of plankton and tiny insects.

Least killifish mate and give birth to live young that are so small they are almost invisible. Fair game to a multitude of predators both large and small, including fish and insects, they must hide among dense vegetation near the surface, away from even their own species.

These smallest creatures of renown in the animal kingdom of North America thrive in ditches and swamps, rivers and springs from South Carolina along the coastal states to New Orleans.

LOGGERHEAD MUSK TURTLE

The loggerhead turtle (*Sternotherus minor minor*) is a bottom creature that appears always to be investigating the crevices and nooks of its spring, day or night. It moves with a slow, deliberate gait and has the posture and mannerisms of a tiny dinosaur as it holds its head erect for a better view, sways it from side to side, arches it out and down when stopping to probe the bottom, then raises it high again noting all surrounding events. Thus the loggerhead roams the spring terrain. Two small barbels visible beneath the lower jaw assist it in detecting the odors of food that vary from carrion to small fish, insects, plants and snails.

The loggerhead has especially well-developed jaw muscles in its large head for crushing the snails abundant in its environment. It lacks teeth, but the prominent sharp cusps of the jaw are capable of cutting and tearing snails or pieces of flesh.

Loggerheads, one of the most abundant spring

turtles, inhabit springs of north-central Florida and slow-moving, clear waters of southern Georgia and southeastern Alabama.

LONGNOSE GAR

The longnose gar (*Lepisosteus osseus*) is a true spring inhabitant only in the larger springs and their rivers. In smaller springs, the gar is a transient hunter, entering springs and runs at night from rivers and lakes in search of its prey. Groups of gars are often visible during the day at the mouth of spring runs maintaining their position in the warm spring water that flows over the top of cooler or more turbid river waters.

Although the gars are not a true schooling species, they will congregate in groups that often number more than a hundred individuals in larger springs. They prefer the quieter waters of large headsprings or large backwater pools of spring rivers, where they hover near the surface or move slowly about their domain. The longnose gar ranges in fresh water, occasionally frequenting brackish water, from southern Quebec west to the Mississippi River system and south to northern Mexico.

The swift gars are like wolves in their springs, hunting in groups and taking whatever small creatures appear vulnerable. They prey primarily upon fish but have been known to take frogs, crayfish, blue crabs and careless small swimming mammals. They will attack as they cruise in groups, or wait singly in ambush, lying motionless at the surface, or they may hide near vegetation, rocks and sunken logs. When they choose their prey, they dart quickly to its side, and with a thrusting sideways lash of their long beaks, impale their prey crosswise on needle-sharp teeth that run the full length of their mouths. They are among the most successful and common predators of the springs as well as of waters throughout most of its range.

Longnose gars spawn in spring; the female followed by a male deposits her adhesive eggs randomly over vegetation. The eggs, if eaten, are toxic to all warm-blooded animals including humans, but not to several species of fishes that prey upon them. The females can be prolific spawners; a Florida female was found to hold more than 77,000 eggs. The eggs hatch quickly, often in less than a week, and young gars emerge with an adhesive pad on their snouts used to attach themselves to vegetation. The young gars grow very rapidly, up to six times faster than the young of other North American freshwater fishes. The females live much longer than the males, reaching ages of 22 years and lengths up to six feet. The males rarely live longer than 11 years.

It is, perhaps, the appearance and abundance of the gars that have caused their unique status among fishes of North America to be overlooked. Gars are living relics of another age. They have changed little in 150 million years. Like the shark, they are so well adapted to the extremes of their environment that they persist through changing millennia.

The flesh of the longnose gar is edible, but nowhere within its range is it particularly utilized. The Seminoles baked the gar in its "shell," and Paleo-Indians used the scales for breast armor and arrowheads. Early American settlers used the scales to cover their wooden plowshares. Gars are presently used in the Mississippi River to propagate an economically important yellow sand-shell mussel. The gars are artificially infected with the larvae of the mussel that harmlessly begin their life cycle in the skin of fish. The exposed gars are then released to distribute the larvae that soon leave the skin of the gars to develop as adult mussels.

MOSQUITOFISH

Just below the surface and not far from vegetation is the realm of the mosquitofish (*Gambusia affinis holbrooki*). They band together to roam back and forth, weaving in and out of floating leaves or between emergent plants. Any small insect larva is likely to fall prey to these fishes. The slightest movement at the surface or on a plant stem attracts their immediate attention.

The females are the more heavy bodied and larger of the sexes and seem content to move casually about, investigating floating debris and searching out insects beneath leaves and sticks. The males live in continuous haste to maintain their harem and ward off the approach of other males.

Mosquitofish differ from most other fishes of the United States in their mode of reproduction. Mosquitofish give birth to living young. The male has a specially modified anal fin with which he fertilizes the female internally. The female carries the eggs until they hatch, and her young emerge alive. The young quickly swim to hide in dense vegetation to avoid predation even from their own species. In Florida, mosquitofish breed throughout the year but less extensively in winter months. The mosquitofish ranges from the east-central United States south to Mexico and is one of the few freshwater fishes regularly inhabiting coastal, brackish waters. Mosquitofish are abundant in springs wherever surface vegetation offers them protection from strong currents and predators. Females are more common, far outnumbering the males. Black coloration, melanism, occurs in both sexes but primarily in the males, giving them striking patterns of black spots and bands, particularly bands across the eye. Mosquitofish closely resemble the common pet store guppy in size and behavior.

MULLET

The torpedo-shaped mullet (*Mugil cephalus*) are ubiquitous nomads of Florida's springs, rivers and coastal waters. Noted for their curious habit of leaping into the air several times in succession, coastal bays and inlets are sometimes invaded by vast schools of leaping mullet.

Mullet are primarily vegetarians that feed on bottom plants and algae. In springs they are easily observed skimming the bottom, taking in mouthfuls of sediment and straining out small plants and occasionally animals. The possess a gizzardlike organ that grinds their food with ingested sand, much like a bird. Their preference for plants requires an unusually long digestive tract — a 13-inch mullet will have a seven-foot intestine.

Mullet are a well-known food fish in Florida. They are caught commercially in nets or with hook and line with dough and meal as bait. They may attain lengths of more than 30 inches and weights to 14 pounds. Mullet range temperate and tropical seas world-wide where they support a major fishery. Mullet are raised for food commercially in Africa, the Middle East and much of the Orient.

PINFISH

Pinfish (*Lagodon rhomboides*) are not common transients to springs, generally invading only large springs near the coast. When they do appear, their stay is relatively short but not likely to go unnoticed. They move across the bottom by the hundreds, feeding continuously on whatever small creatures lie in their path, moving aside native freshwater inhabitants with their invasions.

Pinfish characteristically dominate open, grassy areas around a spring and its river. They rarely are observed entering spring caves or even venturing into the deep waters of a headspring. Their shallow-water preferences in the sea appear to be maintained in the springs.

Pinfish are a major food source for a number of larger saltwater fishes that enter springs. Were pinfish not present, the local populations of freshwater fishes would fall prey to a great number of predacious saltwater assailants.

Pinfish can attain lengths of up to 14 inches, but rarely are visible that large in springs. Pinfish range from Cape Cod south to Florida and west across the Gulf to the Yucatan peninsula.

REDBREAST SUNFISH

The redbreast sunfish (*Lepomis auritus*) ranges throughout Florida's fresh waters, especially in rivers, but its characteristic coloration is more evident in springs. These sunfishes occupy both headsprings and spring runs and often gather in small congregations, mixing with other sunfish species as they wander about their spring. Though the most common sunfish in the Suwannee and Sante Fe rivers, they are one of the least abundant sunfish species in springs, yet they are the most apparent, as they readily approach human visitors to their realms. Among the many inhabitants of springs, the redbreasts venture into deeper waters than most. Small groups have been observed in large headsprings casually feeding at depths of over 100 feet. Aquatic insects comprise their major food source.

The redbreast, like others in the sunfish family, spawns in spring after the male fans a small depression on the bottom in shallow water. The resplendent male then attracts and briefly courts a female. With their spawning completed, he stays to guard the nest and hatching fry. Redbreasts occasionally interbreed with other sunfishes, especially bluegills.

The redbreast sunfish originally occurred in eastern North America from as far north as New Brunswick to the east of the Appalachians, south to central Florida and west to the Apalachicola River. It has since been introduced to Texas and Oklahoma. Recent experimental stocking efforts have introduced the redbreast to Florida rivers west of the Apalachicola. Within its expanding range, the redbreast is a popular sportfish, primarily in the South where it grows to suitable size.

REDEAR SUNFISH

Redear sunfish (*Lepomis microlophus*) are reclusive fishes, spending the majority of time hidden in cover or dense vegetation. Large adult redears ordinarily are not easily approached by divers and rarely allow close observation. But while nest guarding, they are among the first of fish species to attack intruders, including photographers and cameras.

Redears are easily identified by the relatively large size of the adult, the red or orange patch on the gill cover, and the extremely long pointed pectoral fins. The younger redears, equivalent in size to the rest of the bream family, wander about, often joining small bands of bluegills in open areas of springs and runs. Smaller redears generally are silver and lack distinctive coloration except for the red gill patch. Neither adults nor young redears are abundant in small springs and streams.

With snails plentiful in most springs, redears have only to wander and eat them at leisure. The redear's mouth and teeth are well adapted for their fare. Teeth designed for crushing make short work of a snail's shell. Considerable chewing ensues as the meat and shell are separated by the fish's tongue. The meat is then swallowed, and the shell is spit out.

The large size of the redears among other sporting panfish gives them a favored status with anglers throughout the redears' extensive range from Indiana south to Florida and Texas. Florida's record-size redears have, for consecutive years, been taken from panhandle springs.

REDEYE CHUB

Redeye chubs (*Notropis harperi*) are a nomadic species that constantly roam the springs in search of food, darting suddenly and gracefully to capture minute insects and plankton too small for the human eye to see. They rarely venture more than a few feet from their cover as they wander along a spring's perimeter. They are present throughout deep and shallow spring waters but tend to prefer the flowing water of spring runs.

The redeyes' two-inch size makes them vulnerable to a great many larger fishes, and their tight schooling behavior through dense cover constitutes their only margin of safety. It is not yet fully understood how such schooling fishes are led or how their direction is determined, but these minnows display one characteristic that enables them to school as closely as they do. A dark line ending at the base of the tail extends down each side of a minnow. By always keeping the line of another

schooling member in sight as a reference point, and by relying on their sensitivity to movement vibrations, they can effectively move as one large organism. Almost all schooling fishes have distinct lines, bands and spots as aids in protective schooling.

Evasive reactions at detecting odors released by a killed or wounded member of their own species is another survival mechanism used by schooling fishes. The odor warns them of an attack on their species nearby, and the school will avoid the area until the odor dissipates.

RIVER SNAIL

The river snail (*Goniobasis catenaria*) inhabits the springs environment in such abundance that it occurs in virtually all major springs, inhabiting each across its entire sunlit expanse. The environment of the river snail is ideally suited for its tremendous abundance. Food is plentiful, the waters are ideally pure and warm, and the minerals it needs for strong shell growth lie in the limestone comprised already of shells laid down by similar creatures millennia ago.

The river snail is equipped with a special tongue, peculiar to the mollusk family, specially designed for consuming their algal food. A snail's tongue, or "radula," is a ribbonlike organ studded with rows of small teeth and located beneath its muscular body. As the snail moves across leaves and sticks, the radula scrapes the algal film free of the surface to be ingested. A river snail spends a considerable amount of its time grazing, and, as the radula wears with use, it is constantly replaced from behind, much like a human fingernail.

Excavations of Mohican Indian settlements in Virginia and the Carolinas reveal that Mohicans once collected multitudes of these snails for food. Unable to survive in those regions today, the river snail's range has been reduced to springs and calcerous streams of northern Florida and Georgia.

SAILFIN MOLLY

Sailfin mollies (*Poecilia latippina*) occur in both brackish and fresh waters in Florida and maintain breeding populations along the coast as well as in lakes, rivers and streams far inland. Preferring secluded, shallow pools with little or no current, a population of mollies is well removed from the constant predation threat common in more open, accessible environs. Though never free of predation, their reclusive habitat provides security for individuals as they forage for minute insects and plankton independently of their group. Mollies generally swim as a loose congregation roaming near or at the surface, retreating swiftly to the safety of cover when disturbed.

The molly has an extended breeding season lasting six months or more. Like its relatives the mosquitofish and least killifish, the male bears a "gonopodium" — a modified anal fin used to fertilize the females internally. The female gives birth to living young, of which a disproportionate number are females. During the breeding season, a state of fierce competition exists between males as they establish and defend territorial boundaries while endeavoring to attract passing females.

The sailfin molly is an inhabitant of coastal and fresh waters from South Carolina south along the Gulf states to Mexico and California. Through artificial introductions, the molly has expanded its range to California and Hawaii.

SHADOW BASS

Shadow bass (*Ambloplites ariommus*) are limited in range to east- and west-flowing tributaries of the lower Mississippi Valley and rivers along the Gulf to the Florida panhandle. Cool and clear, well-oxygenated, flowing water with cover and shade provided by vegetation are normal habitats of the shadow bass. They have long been thought to be a subspecies of the rock bass, *Ambloplites rupestris*, a common inhabitant of the northeastern United States. New evidence suggests that shadow bass are a separate species.

Shadow bass, like other members of their family, do not attain great size. Lengths of eight inches and weights nearing two pounds are maximum. As predators, their prey varies from insects to smaller fishes. The excellent eating quality of the shadow and rock bass make them popular sportfishes across their range.

Despite the contrasting markings of black and brown splotches and prominent dark red eyes, shadow bass and rock bass are often confused with another member of their family, the warmouth, *Lepomis gulosus*, which occasionally display a similar but less distinctive mottled appearance.

SHEEPSHEAD

Sheepshead (*Archosargus probatocephalus*), like snappers, most often occur in abundance when they enter springs and spring rivers. They are not a schooling species, but tend to remain in loose congregations as they swim slowly near the bottom, stopping often to search for food. They rarely venture far into fresh water. Most sheepshead occur within ten miles of the sea and are most abundant in the headsprings of the Crystal, Chassahowitzka and Homosassa rivers.

Sheepshead are popular sportfish of inshore waters where they can attain lengths of 2 1/2 feet and weights of 30 pounds. Their excellent eating quality is well known throughout their extensive range. Sheepshead are shallow-water fishes, inhabiting the Bay of Fundy south along the Atlantic and Gulf coasts to Brazil.

SOUTHERN BROWN BULLHEAD

Brown bullheads (*Ictalurus nebulosus marmoratus*), like white catfish, are nocturnal fishes that leave their dark sanctuaries at dusk to feed, and return by dawn. Their feeding habits and spawning seasons are also similar to those of the white catfish. Brown bullheads, however, are much deeper penetrators of cave systems. The two species, generally similar in size, are easily distinguished by the obvious mottled coloration of the brown bullhead.

Studies of the brown bullhead have revealed the family of catfishes to have remarkable adaptations in their sense of taste and smell. In addition to a bullhead's barbels and many hundreds of thousands of taste buds in the skin used to locate and identify food, the ability of the nose to detect odor has the fascinating function of determining social behavior.

Brown bullheads, and probably catfishes in general, are able to detect pheromones released by its species that give each individual the capability to literally smell and remember each other. Groups and individuals establish territories and defend them against others of their species detected to be intruders. Within a singular group, a hierarchy develops with one fish dominating. If a stranger enters the group's territory, the subordinates gather around the leader for protection and the leader then engages the intruder in combat.

When bullhead concentrations become dense, their society changes from being territorial to being communal. When high concentrations of pheromones are detected, territories are no longer defended and all aggression ceases.

The brown bullhead of Florida springs, lakes

and rivers is a southern subspecies of the northern bullhead, *Ictalurus nebulosus*. Found from southern Illinois, Oklahoma and Arkansas east to the Carolinas and south to Florida, the southern brown bullhead is distinctly more mottled than its northern relative that ranges from the Dakotas east to Maine and Canada. Because of its excellent eating qualities, the brown bullhead has been widely introduced west of its original range.

SPOTTED BULLHEAD

Spotted bullheads (*Ictalurus serracanthus*) are not a common spring inhabitant, preferring instead the environment of tannic rivers with spring tributaries. They are not an abundant species even there. Almost a Florida endemic, their range is confined to the Suwannee, Apalachicola and Ochlockonee river systems of northern Florida, southern Alabama and Georgia.

Relatively little is known about spotted bullheads. Their behavior and feeding habits appear similar to other species of cave-dwelling catfishes. They move from their cave at dusk, never venturing far from its entrance, to scavenge the spring basin and return to their sanctuaries by dawn. Exceptionally shy and uncomfortable in the beam of bright lights, these colorful fishes don't normally allow close observation and most often retreat deeper into their limestone niches when approached by divers.

Except for the bright yellow spots that mark its sides, the spotted bullhead closely resembles the flathead bullhead, *Ictalurus platycephalous*, which inhabits coastal streams of Virginia and Georgia. The spotted bullhead was long thought to be a subspecies of the flathead bullhead until Florida scientists determined the spotted bullhead to be a distinct species.

SPOTTED SUCKER

The spotted sucker (*Minytrema melanops*), named for the spots located on each of its scales, is one of the more unglamorous and secretive spring creatures. Suckers are relatively common in springs, but populations are higher in Florida's larger rivers. They are dwellers primarily of deeper spring runs where, by day, they group in small schools, rarely venturing far from cover. Schools are occasionally found resting on the bottom in shaded areas, perched on their pectoral fins in similar fashion as darters.

Spotted suckers spawn in early spring in aggregations that frequently become large schools. The males develop a red band of coloration along their sides extending almost the entire length of their bodies. When spawning is completed, they abandon their eggs.

Suckers are noted for their excellent taste in the northern regions of their range where waters are colder, but are rarely eaten in Florida. The spotted sucker is found in larger streams, lakes and rivers from Minnesota eastward, and south to Florida and Texas.

SPOTTED SUNFISH

During spawning, the male spotted sunfish becomes one of the most colorful fishes of the springs. The white trim of its fins brightens, the pelvic fins turn a deep black, and a red sash appears on the upper back. Spotted sunfish (*Lepomis punctatus*) display breeding behavior and seasons similar to the bluegill's, and the two species often build their nests side by side in nesting congregations. The males' bright colors aid in attracting the appropriate mates, but the tendency of the sunfishes to group as they spawn gives rise, nevertheless, to a number of hybrid offspring.

The spotted sunfish inhabit springs, lakes and rivers throughout Florida. The adults are readily observed as they go about their daily rounds and are quick to identify bread at the surface. The young are less visible, remaining with other immature sunfishes in the protection of vegetation and among the snarls of sunken trees and branches.

Spotted sunfish are a popular sportfish in the southeast with a range extending from South Carolina to Florida, west to Texas and the Mississippi Valley. In Florida, their common name of "stumpknocker" may be derived from their tendency to spawn and feed in areas of submerged stumps.

SPRING CRAYFISH

The spring crayfish (*Procambarus speculifer*) represents the most abundant crayfish species occurring in springs and spring-fed rivers of north Florida which, interestingly, comprises the entire extent of its range. It is rarely found outside its preferred waters of flowing, clear, calcerous rivers and springs. Within its limited range, five distinct populations have been discovered, each inhabiting streams and springs of a major river drainage system.

As common as the spring crayfish are, they are rarely visible. They are nocturnal inhabitants, waiting until night before emerging from their caves or vantage points to wander in their dark search for food. Crayfish are primarily scavengers, eating whatever organic material they find including dead and dying larger creatures and occasionally, if food is scarce, each other.

The crayfish of Florida's springs are the largest of their family in the state. Their claws or "chelae" are gnarled with rough, white knobs, and bands of bright red are visible on their flank and tail. These bright colors, when meshed with those of spring algae, limestone and plants, blend to provide the crayfish with excellent camouflage.

That camouflage, along with a sturdy shell and pincer grip, are important tools to these obscure creatures. The crayfish are prey to an assortment of land animals as well as their most common predators — the basses.

In the uncommon event a crayfish is caught in the open by a marauding bass, the crayfish reveals a formidable mechanism of defense. The approach of a predator causes the crayfish to tuck its tail, lean back, and wave its wide-spread pincers at the intruder. As the predator attempts to circle behind, the crayfish follows in turn, keeping its chelae waving at its enemy. Most potential predators are discouraged and leave. But as a last resort, the crayfish may suddenly leave the bottom and swim blindly backwards at surprising speed, propelled by its muscular tail. Larger basses will on occasion take a whole crayfish and quickly attempt to turn it around tail-first to swallow it. Unless the bass is very quick in that maneuver, the pinching, flailing crayfish usually escapes to live another day.

STINKPOT TURTLE

The stinkpot (*Sternotherus odoratus*) of Florida's springs is easily identified by the light streaks on its head and its relatively small size, which rarely exceeds 4 1/2 inches. Its shell is commonly covered with a species of green filamentous algae that grows only on the shells of turtles. They can be observed day and night roaming spring terrains searching out insects, snails, algae and carrion.

Courtship and mating for the stinkpot is sporadic throughout the year, but peaks in spring and fall. Their matings take place underwater under cover of darkness. Females leave the water to lay two to four eggs in nests dug in the ground, usually beneath logs and hollow stumps. They often find and use the same nests as other female stinkpots.

Upon emerging from their nest, hatching turtles are known to be able to distinguish colors and orient their immediate migration to water by walking toward open areas which reflect the brightest light. Hatchling turtles are vulnerable to a number of predators, including the basses, bullfrogs and snakes.

The stinkpot is a common resident in springs as well as in clear, shallow waters of lakes, rivers, and streams. The stinkpot has an extensive range, occurring from New England to southern Ontario, south to Florida and west to Wisconsin and Texas. One stinkpot residing in the Philadelphia Zoological Gardens lived for 53 years.

STRIPED BASS

Striped bass (*Morone saxatilis*), are anadromous, oceanic fishes that begin their life cycle in fresh water. Unlike the anadromous salmon, they spawn more than once, though not necessarily every year. Female bass deposit their eggs and leave them to drift in river currents. The uncertainty of egg survival requires spawning a great number of eggs; a large female will carry more than three million.

Striped bass as adults in fresh water are ravenous carnivores that consume a variety of fishes, crustaceans, invertebrates and insects. They rarely eat steadily as most fishes but tend to gorge themselves and then stop feeding until their meal is completely digested. When feeding does occur, individuals of a school feed simultaneously. The largest striped bass ever reported were caught in 1891 in North Carolina where several weighed 125 pounds each.

As an oceanic species, striped bass are coastal fishes seldom found more than a few miles from shore except during spring and fall migrations. Their original range spans the North American Atlantic coast from the St. Lawrence River in Canada south to the St. Johns River in Florida. Others occur in the Gulf of Mexico in fresh and brackish tributaries in western Florida, Alabama, Mississippi and Louisiana. In 1879 and 1882 they were introduced in the Pacific coast and now range from Oregon to southern California.

SUWANNEE BASS

The Suwannee bass (*Micropterus notius*) is a popular gamefish in Florida within its uniquely limited range. It is the only known species of fish restricted to the Suwannee and Ochlockonee river systems.

The Suwannee bass is often confused with the largemouth bass in Florida, but differs from it in a number of respects. The smaller Suwannee bass rarely exceeds 16 inches in length and prefers more confined and swifter waters than the largemouth.

The Suwannee bass belongs to one of two defined groups of basses that inhabit Florida. Along with the Suwannee bass, one group also includes the spotted bass and redeye bass of Florida's panhandle. The basses of this group differ from the other by having an upper jaw that, in adults, does not extend beyond their eye. The basses of the other group, which includes the Florida largemouth and northern largemouth, are larger and adults have an upper jaw that extends back beyond the eye.

Aside from its smaller size and relatively smaller mouth, the Suwannee bass differs little in attitude and skill as an aquatic predator. Although it is known to take whatever smaller creatures its size allows, crayfish are the principal prey. Spawning seasons and behaviors of the Suwannee bass coincide with those of its larger and more common relatives.

SUWANNEE COOTER

Suwannee cooters (*Chrysemys conciuna suwanniensis*) are one of the most abundant turtles of springs, either in or out of the water. Cooters are notably fond of basking and spend much of the midday hours in the sun. Frequently, 20 or 30 cooters can be seen sharing the same log. Their active periods are usually early morning and late afternoon when they graze on the vegetation that comprises most of their diet. Suwannee cooters are one of the few purely grazing turtles in the world.

The cooter species are wary aquatic turtles but have an unexplainable tendency to wander, a venture that often proves fatal when they cross roads, encounter predators or become overheated by the sun. Studies of these unusual travels indicate that cooters navigate by the sun when they journey overland.

A female cooter also leaves the water at least twice a year to lay her eggs. Small nests are dug in soft earth with her hind feet. She lays an average of 17 to 19 eggs in the nest and then covers them to incubate for two to three months, depending on the soil temperature. The vulnerable hatchlings, upon emerging from the ground, instinctively move toward water and a number of waiting predators that include mammals, birds, snakes and alligators. Those that survive this gauntlet to water have survived their most hazardous overland venture.

Suwannee cooters are almost uniquely euryhaline turtles, inhabiting spring-fed rivers and springs of north and central Florida, as well as saltwater turtlegrass flats off river mouths along the Gulf Coast. They share the spring habitat with three other cooter species to which they bear close resemblance.

Cooters have derived their unusual name from the word "kuta," a word for turtle in several African dialects brought to America in the early days of slavery. In the Mississippi Valley, they are known as "sliders."

TADPOLE MADTOM

The tadpole madtom (*Noturus gyrinus*) is a common resident of lakes and slow-flowing rivers of the eastern United States and southern Canada. In Florida, tadpole madtoms search the spring bottom at night for plankton and immature insects. Their small size combined with their desirability as prey to many fishes has made the madtom a common bait species. They have been reported to be prey even to garter snakes.

WHITE CATFISH

White catfish (*Ictalurus catus*) in springs are primarily nocturnal fishes residing by day in the dark reaches and twilight areas of caves, crevices or shaded recesses of their domain. Swimming deep enough into cave systems to escape direct view of bright light, they seek quiet sand areas protected from strong currents to wait for night. At dusk they move from their caves to scavenge the spring bottom for food.

The catfishes are aided in their nightly food forays by barbels sensitive to taste that extend from around their mouths and drag across the bottom. They are omnivorous fishes feeding occasionally upon plants and whatever carrion, small fishes, worms and insects they encounter.

Spawning occurs through the summer and begins with a nest depression fanned in the bottom, usually near the protection of a stump, cliff wall, bank or log. With the nest completed, the male and female caress one another with the barbels, settle over the nest and deposit eggs and milt. Their rituals continue until the female is spent of eggs. One or both parents remain with the eggs, fanning them with fins and moving them around the nest with barbels and fin spines.

The eggs hatch in approximately a week, and the young emerge from the nest in a black, roving cloud herded by an adult. An adult, usually the male, will shepherd its school containing hundreds of fry for several weeks before the young finally disperse. The young with undeveloped protective fin spines fall prey to many predators including other catfishes, water snakes, turtles and basses. Adult catfish are relatively predation-free.

White catfish are present in coastal streams and rivers from Chesapeake Bay south along the Atlantic and Gulf coasts to Texas. Lengths of up to two feet and excellent edibility make them a desirable food fish across their range that now includes, through introduction, the Pacific coast states.

APPENDIX B
CAVE DIVING SAFETY

Recognizing the unique hazards of Florida's underwater cave environment, and that no amount of open-water training or experience can prepare a diver for a safe cave dive, the National Association of Cave Diving (NACD) was founded in 1968. Aimed at the recreational diver, its mandate remains to certify divers in safe cave-diving procedures and cave ecosystem conservation.

In 1978, the Cave Diving Section of the National Speleological Society (NSS/CDS) was formed with the same mandate aimed at cave explorers using diving as a tool in their explorations.

Today, the NACD and NSS/CDS train divers with three minimum requirements critical to safely entering Florida's underwater caves. First, a dive team must carry an unwinding reel of safety line that is a single continuous guide back to open water. Air consumption rules have evolved to the "Rule of One-Thirds" — when the first member of a team uses one-third of his/her air supply, the team exits the cave system with two-thirds of their air remaining as a reserve for the return journey, potential emergencies or decompression. And no diver using compressed air should exceed the established maximum sport diving depth of 130 feet.

With safety the maximum concern, important distinctions unique to this environment have evolved for equipment and training required to dive in Florida's springs and caves.

A "Spring Diver" is open-water certified, dives in a zone with no overhead obstructions, and uses basic open-water diving equipment with daylight the only source of light. For Spring Divers in all state parks and most commercial diving springs, a "no light rule" is enforced. To prevent inexperienced divers from entering areas where advanced training is required, underwater lights cannot be carried by Spring Divers.

A "Cavern Diver" has completed a training course and dives a zone where an overhead ceiling is present but surface light is still visible. Additional equipment of two underwater lights and a safety line reel is required. Maximum depth and horizontal penetration limits are set and vary according to certifying agency.

After an extensive training course, a "Cave Diver" dives a zone of total darkness in a complex tunnel system where extensive extra equipment is required. Three underwater lights, two knives and a submersible dive table or dive computer are required per diver in addition to three safety line reels, one of which holds up to 400 feet, plus a gap line reel for attaching to the primary lines already in place. Advanced cave divers most often use double tanks for extended time underwater and wear dry suits for extra warmth.

Florida has a prolific number of spring caves and sinks, some of them among the deepest known underwater caves in the Western Hemisphere. They are gradually being explored and mapped ever further by a new kind of emerging "high tech" cave diver using new technology and breathing mixed gas combinations that allow for dives of record duration and depth. When new record depth and distance underwater explorations are made, it will be in this environment found in the depths of the Floridan Aquifer.

References

For the reader interested in knowing more about how to find and travel on Florida's springs, an annual state park guidebook can be obtained from the Florida Park Service, and the following two books are especially recommended:

Carter, Elizabeth F., & J. L. Pearch. 1985. *A Canoeing and Kayaking Guide to the Streams of Florida.* Volume 1. Birmingham: Menasha Ridge Press.

DeLoach, Ned. 1991. *Divers Guide to Underwater Florida.* Jacksonville: New World Publications.

For more detailed historical and biological information, the following books are recommended:

Bartram, William. 1928. *The Travels of William Bartram.* Dover.

Burgess, Robert F. 1976. *The Cave Divers.* New York: Dodd, Mead and Co.

Carr, Archie. 1952. *The Handbook of Turtles.* Ithaca: Comstock Publishing Associates.

Conant, Roger. 1958, 1975. *A Field Guide to Reptiles and Amphibians of Eastern and Central North America.* Boston: Houghton Mifflin.

Hartman, Daniel Stanwood. 1971. *Behavior and Ecology of the Florida Manatee.* PhD thesis, Cornell University.

Lane, Ed. 1986. *Karst in Florida.* Special Publication No. 29. Tallahassee: Florida Geological Survey.

Lee, David S., Carter Gilbert, Charles Hocutt, Robert Jenkins, Don McAllister, and Jay Stauffer, Jr. 1980. *Atlas of North American Freshwater Fishes.* Publication 1980 - 82, North Carolina Biological Survey. North Carolina State Museum of Natural History.

Pritchard, Peter C. H. 1978. "Fishes." In *Rare and Endangered Biota of Florida* (Vol. 4), Carter R. Gilbert, Editor. Gainesville: University Presses of Florida.

Prosser, Joe, & H. J. Grey, Editors. 1992. *NSS Cave Diving Manual.* Branford, Florida: The Cave Diving Section of the National Speleological Society, Inc.

Reynolds, John E., and Daniel K. Odell. 1991. *Manatees and Dugongs.* New York: Facts on File.

Roseman, Jack C., G. L. Faulkner, C. W. Hendry, Jr., and R. W. Hull. 1977. *Springs of Florida.* Bulletin 31 revised. Tallahassee: Florida Department of Natural Resources and U.S. Geological Survey.

Stone, William C., Editor. 1993. *The Wakulla Springs Project.* Gaithersburg, MD: The U.S. Deep Diving Team.

Webb, S. David, Editor. 1974. *Pleistocene Mammals of Florida.* Gainesville: The University Presses of Florida.

INDEX

Note: Photographs are indicated by bold typeface; photographs of species are indexed by common name only.